HE+

Gower College Swansea

Gorseinon : Swansea : SA4 6RD Tel: (01792) 890731
This resource is **YOUR RESPONSIBILITY** and is due for
return/renewal on or before the last date shown.

John Farndon, a graduate of Jesus College, Cambridge, is the author of many books on contemporary issues, including *China Rises* and *India Booms* (Virgin), and *Bird Flu* and *Iran* in the 'Everything You Need to Know' series (Icon). He also writes widely for children, including the bestselling *Do Not Open* (Dorling Kindersley), and has been short-listed four times for the Junior Science Book Prize.

www.john-farndon-books.co.uk

Libby Purves OBE is a radio presenter, journalist and author. Best known for presenting BBC Radio Four's *Midweek*, she also writes regularly for *The Times* and has published twelve novels. She is a graduate of St Anne's College, Oxford, with a First in English Language and Literature.

—THE OXBRIDGE QUESTIONS—

DO YOU THINK YOU'RE CLEVER?

JOHN FARNDON
INTRODUCTION BY LIBBY PURVES

ICON BOOKS

Published in the UK in 2009 by
Icon Books Ltd, Omnibus Business Centre,
39–41 North Road, London N7 9DP
email: info@iconbooks.co.uk
www.iconbooks.co.uk

Sold in the UK, Europe, South Africa and Asia
by Faber & Faber Ltd, Bloomsbury House,
74–77 Great Russell Street, London WC1B 3DA
or their agents

Distributed in the UK, Europe, South Africa and Asia
by TBS Ltd, TBS Distribution Centre, Colchester Road,
Frating Green, Colchester CO7 7DW

Published in Australia in 2009
by Allen & Unwin Pty Ltd,
PO Box 8500, 83 Alexander Street,
Crows Nest, NSW 2065

Distributed in Canada by
Penguin Books Canada,
90 Eglinton Avenue East, Suite 700,
Toronto, Ontario M4P 2YE

ISBN: 978-184831-083-4

Typesetting in 11pt Plantin by Marie Doherty

Printed and bound in the UK by
CPI Mackays, Chatham ME5 8TD

Introduction
by Libby Purves

When you ask someone questions, especially in an interview whose outcome matters, you are checking up on two things. One is the person's knowledge – simple enough to gauge – but the other is more nebulous. You want to know *how* they think: what sort of engine their mind is, whether it runs neatly on logical rails, or soars high above every topic with the eyes of an eagle. Or perhaps, whether it just hops about like a drunken bunny-rabbit (my own *modus operandi*, all too often). Whether you're going to teach that candidate at a university or offer them a job, you need to know this. You need to get a sense of how they approach the unexpected.

So that's the questioner's perspective; and the questioner of course has the advantage of surprise and authority. The interviewee, on the other hand, may simply stare and sweat, temporarily deprived of the power of speech by sheer amazement. Some have displayed a legendary cool: confronted with the philosopher's favourite opening 'Is this a question?' one lad supposedly replied with a languid yawn, 'Well, if this is an answer, I suppose it must have been, mustn't it?' Most of us wouldn't be up to that. Or not that quickly. Indeed technical knowledge, acquired by rote through years of plodding school exams can even prove a bit of an impediment. You can be a competent electrical engineering student and still be floored by someone asking

'Can a thermostat think?' Yet your answer, if you stay calm and thoughtful, might well betray a deeper and more useful understanding of thermostats to run alongside your technical expertise.

Similarly, you may stutter helplessly when asked 'Are you a novel or a poem?'; but if you can get your mind into a flexible, relaxed state your answer will show it. Even if you just say 'Frankly, I think I'm halfway between a rap lyric and a technical manual' they'll know that you have a degree of self-knowledge. And if asked to 'describe a spoon to a Martian', a relaxed mind will tell you (as it tells the author of this book) that before you answer you will have to decide on the physique of your Martian, and whether he can see or hear or understand the concept of grasping a tool. If the Martian is a mere brain encased in rock, there will be a bit more work to do: you'll have to explain fingers before you come on to the spoon …

Actually, questions about explaining things to Martians are always my favourites, because they remind us that there is no use at all being eloquent and stylish and clever and knowledgeable if you are at the same time crashingly insensitive to your audience and what they will relate to. All novelists, broadcasters and teachers need to have that lesson stamped in their DNA.

And yet there is value in such questions, and in all the unsettling ones John offers in this book. No single discipline, after all, is ever enough to make a rounded, curious, exploring human being. Physicists need to think philosophically, philosophers to acknowledge solid realities; historians, medics and mathematicians all have to work in guesstimates from time to time, if only to run a mental double-check on their empirical findings.

Daily common sense is a useful thing, but can also be limiting: if somebody asks you how to weigh your own head, or whether you can light a candelabra in a space shuttle, it's fruitless to snap back, 'Why on earth would I want to?' Though that might, I suppose, ramp you up a notch or two in a more sternly pragmatic contest like *The Apprentice*.

Interviewers – especially in the ancient universities – get a lot of stick for asking apparently crazy questions. I think we should cut them some slack. There is no evidence that those who deal best with weird questions always get in, and certainly this book is not offered as a magical short-cut to winning prestigious places or indeed jobs. But it pays tribute to that style of thinking, and illustrates some ways of answering particular questions. The answers are not 'models' or cribs; merely examples of how this author would approach them. Personally, I am happy to say that I disagree with one or two of his conclusions; but the very process of disagreeing has been entertaining and stimulating.

For by and large, it's not only useful trying to answer these deceptively potty questions, but fun. Just as it's fun (on a good day) to attempt to answer small children's piercing enquiries about why our noses aren't the other way up, or what a cow is thinking. If we can overcome the terror of the unexpected, such questions give us space to play: to bat around aspects of logic and meaning, and snatch little bits of knowledge from the far corners of our minds and knit them together in a new pattern. It's good to know how to pause without panic, and think without confusion. Think of them as five-finger exercises on the piano of your brain – and disagree as much as you like.

Libby Purves
London 2009

Do You Think You're Clever?

I'm starting to think …

This book is a collection of questions and answers. The questions, of course, are a selection of some of the infamously bizarre and challenging questions put by Oxbridge admissions tutors to potential candidates. The idea is to help them spot the really smart students, the ones who can think on their feet. What's extraordinary about these questions is just how brilliantly thought-provoking they are. You don't have to be an Oxbridge candidate at all to have your mind instantly set whirring by a question such as 'What books are bad for you?', 'Does a Girl Scout have a political agenda?' and 'What happens when you drop an ant?'

Most of the time we saunter through life without thinking much at all. There's no need to, really. Each of us has a store of knowledge and experience that delivers a response automatically with the minimum of effort, and most of the time that automatic response is fine. But the questions in this book won't allow that. They are surprising, intriguing, strange, silly and even downright irritating at times, but what they all have in common is that they invite you to think. And that's so rare that it provokes instant delight. When I've tried some of these questions with my friends, they first burst out laughing, then can't stop coming up with ideas.

I think we humans actually love thinking. It's exciting. It makes us feel alive. Look at all the people busily doing Su Doku and crosswords and quizzes, yet even those are routine. The wonderful thing about these questions is just how many different ways of thinking they open up. Indeed, there is no 'right' answer to any of them. Some of them seem impossible to answer at first, but it's amazing how by pulling in a little scrap of knowledge here, a little bit of logic there and a large dollop of playfulness you can actually come up with a decent answer – or come up with a really intriguing reason why not!

The answers here, of course, are mine. They are not meant to be answers a student could give. They are not even the answers I would necessarily give if put in an interview situation. There seemed no point in trying to recapture the mind frozen with fear under pressure! They are certainly not intended to be 'right' answers. Indeed, I'm sure some Oxbridge tutors will throw up their hands in despair at some of my ideas. The answers here are merely meant to be food for thought – suggestions of ways in which the questions could be answered, and just what they mean.

Each question is different, and each provokes a differ-ent kind of answer. On the whole, I have tried to keep my answers here as neutral as possible, to leave you, the reader, more room for thought. There are a few questions for which a personalised answer was unavoidable, though. On the whole, too, I've tried to answer the questions directly rather than being cleverly evasive, even though that can be wonderfully entertaining and inventive. When asked 'How would you use a barometer to measure the height of a tower block?' the late, great Clement Freud, knowing the answer that was expected all along, apparently came up with a brilliantly silly array of alternatives, such as dropping the barometer from the top and timing its fall, offering it as a bribe to the hall porter to get him to tell you the height, and so on. The correct, and ultimately more interesting answer is, of course, that you measure the air pressure at the top and bottom of the building and find the height from the pressure difference. On the whole, I've given that kind of answer, so that you are free to be as outrageously inventive as you wish.

There's certainly no recipe for answering these questions. Journalists who've focused on these questions say they're about 'lateral thinking', after Edward de Bono's famous 1967 book, *The Use of Lateral Thinking*. Unlike standard 'critical thinking' which merely seeks to evaluate the truth of a statement, 'lateral thinking' is about using statements as spurs to help create entirely new, perhaps unrelated ideas. Because our thinking tends to run along tramlines, de Bono argued, we need tools to provoke us to think in entirely different directions. One example of how this works would be to generate new ideas for say, an ad campaign, by finding a word at random in the dictionary and seeing what new thoughts that provoked about the ad. Such techniques can be effective.

But these questions aren't just about lateral thinking. Some indeed are. You have to think laterally, for instance, to work out how to weigh your head. But many others are simply about thinking for yourself. Some challenge your preconceptions. Some ask you to think about issues that face the world. Some ask you about why things are as they are in our society. Some even ask you fundamental questions about the nature of reality and existence. Some just want your opinion.

I would say the key thing in answering these questions is to stop for a moment and think what the question means, or better still, what *else* the question means. The least interesting, least clever response is the one that comes automatically. The chances are, too, that this is going to subtly miss the point of the question. When asked 'What books are bad for you?' for example, it would be so easy to slip into a clichéd list of morally dubious books – and you could possibly make that interesting by the way you justify your choice. But isn't it worth exploring the question a little further – like for instance, what's meant by 'bad'?

There are some questions such as 'What percentage of the world's water is there in a cow?' and 'What is the population of Croydon?' that seem to require specialist knowledge. If you know the answer, that's great, but what's really intriguing, and really 'clever', is arriving at an answer without any specific knowledge whatsoever. The amazing thing is that this isn't quite so hard to do as you might think. You just need to keep a clear head and marshal the few small things that you do know in the right way.

We got the title of this book, *Do You Think You're Clever?*, from one of the Oxbridge questions and it seemed apt. Answering these questions is about being clever – astonishingly, amusingly, stimulatingly, irritatingly, deviously, mischievously, profoundly, brilliantly clever. But that's something that everyone can be. It's not about knowledge. It's not even about education. It's about bending and twisting your thoughts in all kinds of intriguing ways. And that's something everyone can do. It's not the exclusive territory of those lucky enough to gain their place at Oxbridge, either. There's no bigger obstacle to genuine cleverness than smugness.

The Questions

Do you think you're clever?   **19**

What happens when I drop an ant?   **22**

Why is the pole vaulting world record about 6.5 metres and why can't it be broken?   **24**

If you could go back in time to any period of history, when would it be and why?   **26**

Are you cool?   **29**

If there was an omnipotent god, would he be able to create a stone that he couldn't lift?   **32**

Should someone sell their kidney?   **33**

Is it moral to hook up a psychopath (whose only pleasure is killing) to a reality-simulating machine so that he can believe he is in the real world and kill as much as he likes?   **37**

Should obese people have free NHS treatment?   **40**

Why did they used to make the mill chimneys so tall?   **42**

Why can't you light a candle in a spaceship?   **44**

If I could fold this paper an infinite number of times, how many times must I fold it to reach the moon?   **47**

Can history stop the next war?   **49**

Where does honesty fit into law?   **53**

What books are bad for you?   **58**

What would happen if you drilled through the earth all the way to the other side and then jumped into the hole?   **63**

Does a Girl Scout have a political agenda?   **65**

What does it mean to be happy?   **69**

Smith sees Jones walking towards a cliff. Smith knows Jones is blind but doesn't like him, so allows him to walk off the edge. Is this murder?   **73**

How would you measure the weight of your own head?   **75**

What is fate?   **77**

How would you describe an apple?   **82**

The stage: a platform for opinions or just entertainment – what are your thoughts?   **86**

I am an oil baron in the desert and I need to deliver oil to four different towns which happen to lie in a straight line. I must visit each town in turn, returning to my oil tank between each visit. Where should I position my tank to drive the shortest possible distance? Roads are no problem, since I have a sheikh friend who will build me as many roads as I like for free.   **89**

Think of a painting of a tree. Is the tree real?   **93**

Does a snail have a consciousness?   **96**

Why is there salt in the sea?   **100**

What is the point of using NHS money to keep old people alive? **103**

You have a 3-litre jug and a 5-litre jug. Make 4 litres. **107**

Was it fair that a woman's planning application for painting her door purple in a conservation area was declined? **109**

Do you think Chairman Mao would have been proud of the China of today? **114**

Why isn't there a global government? **118**

Is the Bible a fictional work? Could it be called chick lit? **125**

Is feminism dead? **128**

What percentage of the world's water is contained in a cow? **134**

If you're not in California, how do you know it exists? **136**

When are people dead? **140**

Chekhov's great, isn't he? **143**

What is the population of Croydon? **148**

Why are big, fierce animals so rare? **151**

Are there too many people in the world? **153**

How many animals did Moses take on the Ark? **157**

How many grains of sand are there in the world? **160**

Was Romeo impulsive? **163**

How would you describe a human to a person from Mars? **167**

What do you like most about the brain? **170**

Why do so few Americans believe in evolution? **173**

How would you reduce crime through architecture? **176**

Would you say greed is good or bad? **179**

If my friend locks me in a room and says I am free to come out whenever I like as long as I pay £5, is this a deprivation of liberty? **183**

How would you travel through time? **186**

Can a computer have a conscience? **190**

What would happen if the Classics department burned down? **193**

Don't you think Hamlet *is a bit long? Well I do.* **195**

Is there such a thing as 'race'? **199**

Is nature natural? **202**

Is the environment a bigger crisis than poverty/AIDS etc? **207**

Why do the words 'God' and 'I' have capital letters? **209**

Is it more important to focus on poverty at home or poverty abroad? **211**

What makes you think I'm having thoughts? **216**

Do you think you're clever? *(Law, Cambridge)*

This is really a tormentor of a question! Answer, modestly, 'no' and of course the interviewer might take you at your word and deny you a place at Oxbridge where, naturally, only clever people are admitted (so rumour has it). Answer 'yes' and you risk suggesting that you are really quite a fool. For a start, the interviewer is bound to be, by virtue of his position (on the other side of the interview), cleverer than you – and by suggesting you might be on his level, you are heading for a fall! And for another thing, anyone who has too much certainty of their own cleverness is unlikely to be wise, or even open enough to learn, which is what, of course, the best students must do. And yet, if you hedge your bets with a non-committal answer, you look like someone who is too vacillating and lacking incisiveness to be an Oxbridge star …

Ever since the days of Ancient Greece, being clever has had rather negative overtones. Cleverness, according to Aristotle, was the mere capacity for figuring out how to achieve something, without the attending touchstone of virtue. It was impossible, he thought, to be wise without being good as well as clever. Plato was equally scathing, saying: 'Ignorance of all things is an evil neither terrible nor excessive, nor yet the greatest of all; but great cleverness and much learning, if they be accompanied by a bad training, are a much greater misfortune.' Ever since, cleverness has had the image of being a rather dubious quality, linked with underhand cunning on one side and braggadocio on the other. Milton's Satan was dubbed 'clever'. So was Mary Shelley's Frankenstein. The devil may be clever, but only angels are wise.

So admitting that you are clever can be tantamount to announcing that you are either devious or a braggart – or even a fool because no one who was wise would believe that they were clever, and no one who was really clever would openly admit to being clever. As Rochefoucauld says, 'It is great cleverness to know when to conceal one's cleverness'. In a hugely pompous tract on *Great Works of Art and what makes them great*, dating from 1925, F.W. Ruckstull summed up the general attitude to displays of cleverness: 'Manet might have become a great artist, but moral myopia doomed him to remain in the ranks of trivial though clever craftsmen.' So that's Manet for you ... Even the brilliant Oscar Wilde had to announce his cleverness with self-deprecating wit, saying, 'I am so clever that sometimes I don't understand a single word of what I'm saying', which is probably the perfect answer to the question.

Of course, if the question had asked, 'Do you think you're intelligent?' I might answer in a different way. Intelligence has far fewer of the negative overtones of cleverness. Cleverness is competitive. Intelligence has an image of objectivity. Yet actually, there are almost as many problems, because there is no universally agreed way of defining what intelligence is or of measuring it. Intelligence tests now have only a little more credibility than Trivial

Pursuit as true measures of intelligence, because they have been shown to be so much influenced by coaching – and the range of tests, too, is so culturally dependent. So if you were to be asked 'Do you think you're intelligent?' and you answered, 'Yes, I have an IQ of 155', the tutor would be more likely to recommend you join Mensa than an Oxbridge college.

Of course, despite all this, my interviewer might be bowled over by the sheer panache of a candidate who said, 'Yes, I'm as clever as you want me to be' and then proceeded to demonstrate it with the wit of Cyrano de Bergerac celebrating his nose. After all, the clever minds of Oxbridge are already doomed to be viewed with some suspicion and envy, so why wouldn't they welcome someone who was prepared to revel in the very thing that marks them out? According to Wordsworth's niece Elizabeth in a little ditty from 1890, the die is cast anyway:

If all the good people were clever
And all clever people were good,
The world would be nicer than ever
We thought that it possibly could.
But somehow it's seldom or never
The two get along as they should.
The good are so harsh to the clever,
The clever so rude to the good.

What happens when I drop an ant?

(Physics, Oxford)

You could answer this question in all kinds of ways – the humorous and human, the absurdly trivial or the grandly existential. But this was a physics question, so it makes sense here to address the science of formicine precipitation.

The first answer, then, might be to say that the ant, which if it's the wingless kind can't fly, falls to the ground – accelerating earthwards as it's pulled down by the mutual gravitational attraction between the ant and the earth. Splat. But there is more to it than that. Ants are so small and light that their fall is considerably slowed on the way down by air resistance – by the collision of the ant with countless air molecules. So while a human skydiver can reach a maximum, or 'terminal', velocity of, say, 50–90 m/s, most ants are so light that their terminal velocity is slow enough for them to drift earthwards gently and for them to survive both the speed of the fall and the impact with the ground.

In fact, recent research in tropical Peru has shown that wingless worker ants are among the world's flying, or rather gliding, animals. When an ant is dropped, it first tumbles vertically. But like a skydiver in the first stages of freefall, it splays its legs to increase drag and gain control. Eventually, by moving its legs to control direction through drag, it eases into a gentle glide at about 4 m/s. It apparently glides backwards because its hindlegs are longer than its forelegs.

The physics doesn't stop here, though, because even in a simple action like dropping an ant, there is a complex assemblage of forces, reactions and consequences. We must remember, for instance, that gravity is a mutual force. So when you drop an ant it might fall towards the ground, but at the same time the earth is moving upwards to meet the ant. Of course, the mass of the ant is so small and the mass of the earth so great that the movement of the earth is immeasurably small, but we can be sure from other fine measurements that it really does happen. Moreover, as Newton's Third Law of Motion makes clear, there is an equal opposite reaction to every action. So the act of dropping the ant will have its own, undetectably small, kickback on your hand.

And as we talk about undetectably small movements, we are reminded of chaos theory and Edward Lorenz's famous suggestion that 'the flap of a butterfly's wings in Brazil sets off a tornado in Texas' – as the tiny movement of the air caused by the butterfly's wings sets in train an escalating, multiplying whirl of movements in the air that culminates in a tornado far away. So, even such a small-scale event as dropping an ant could have manifold unpredictable consequences on every scale from the minuscule to the gigantic. So, actually, it's impossible to say, on a certain level, what happens when you drop an ant.

Einstein's General Theory of Relativity adds another aspect to this seemingly trivial event. Einstein explained gravity as working through the distortion of the fabric of spacetime. So even a small movement of mass – the mass of the ant towards the earth – will minutely alter the fabric of spacetime. And of course the movement of the ant and the movement of the earth will, as Einstein's Special Theory of Relativity shows, cause an (unimaginably small) shift in the time relation between you and the ant …

Ultimately, it all depends on what you want to know.

Why is the pole vaulting world record about 6.5 metres and why can't it be broken? (Computer Science, Cambridge)

Even a kangaroo can't get very high from a standing jump. That's why both conventional high-jumpers and pole-vaulters use a run-up. Instead of accelerating against gravity from zero, the jumper uses the momentum of the run-up to boost upward acceleration. The vaulter's pole enables the maximum possible momentum to be converted into upward acceleration. In terms of physics, it uses the leverage of the pole to convert the kinetic energy of the sprint run-up to combat gravity, or more specifically gravitational potential energy. And it's in the physics that the limits to the heights that can be achieved by a pole-vaulter lie.

Ideally, a vaulter would convert all the kinetic energy of his sprint into vertical acceleration to combat gravity. Of course, in practice, even if he achieves the perfect lift-off some energy will be lost to friction and in things such as the bending of the pole. So pole construction and design is important. Nonetheless, it is possible to calculate the maximum height a vaulter could reach in the ideal circumstances. The limit ultimately depends on the run-up speed.

You can calculate the maximum kinetic energy the vaulter has available from his mass (that is, his body weight) and his velocity, using the formula: half mass times the velocity squared, or $KE = \frac{1}{2}mv^2$. You can calculate, too, the gravitational potential energy that it has to be converted into using the formula: the acceleration due to gravity times the vaulter's mass times the height, or $PE = gmh$, where $g = 9.8$ m/s^2. The vaulter's mass appears on both sides of the equation, and so cancels out. And so you can say the maximum height the vaulter can reach is half of the square of his velocity when divided by the acceleration due to gravity, $h = (\frac{1}{2}v^2/g)$. You'd have to make small adjustments according to the vaulter's own height and centre of mass, but this way you can get a very rough figure of the height the vaulter could potentially reach.

Experts suggest the best that vaulters will ever achieve is about 6.4 metres, because of the limits to their run-up speed. The world record currently stands at 6.14 metres, set by Ukrainian Sergey Bubka on 31 July 1994. Altogether, just seventeen men have ever exceeded 6 metres in a vault. Women, who are generally shorter and able to reach slower run-up speeds, can vault less high. Just one woman, Yelena Isinbayeva, has ever exceeded 5 metres, and experts think the highest that women vaulters are likely to reach is about 5.3 metres.

If you could go back in time to any period of history, when would it be and why? (Law, Oxford)

Who would not jump at the chance to go back even to yesterday, to live moments of your own life again, and see if with hindsight things could and would have been different? And who could resist the astounding opportunities offered by a Tardis voyage into deeper history? To step into, or even to catch a fleeting glimpse of the real, living, breathing, happening long-lost world of the past would be such a glorious, heart-stopping piece of magic that you'd take whatever was offered without worrying about choice. How amazing it would be to watch the dramatic highlights of history as an eyewitness – Julius Caesar riding triumphant into Rome to be proclaimed emperor, Queen Elizabeth I greeting the heroes of the English fleet after the defeat of the Spanish Armada. And yet wouldn't the quiet, unnoticed passing of life in the backwaters be just as riveting – whether you dropped in on a medieval peasant waking tired as always for a day's work in the fields or eavesdropped on an eighteenth-century housemaid meeting her lover for a tryst between shifts. Just give me that time ticket and I'll take it to anywhere!

But a specific choice is requested. I could go back in time simply for the personal pleasure of witnessing something such as Mozart in concert at first-hand. That would indeed be extraordinary. And yet perhaps ultimately only a little more comes from this than watching a really good DVD. What if stepping back into the past gave you the almost godlike opportunity to change the course of history with the benefit of hindsight? Then, it would be unimaginably wasteful not to try.

Maybe, for instance, I could go back to Sarajevo on the morning of 28 June 1914 and warn the Bosnian police to keep Gavrilo Princip away from the Archduke Franz Ferdinand, whose assassination by Princip later that day triggered the events that led to the First World War of 1914–18. Perhaps that one small intervention might have averted the First World War – the most horrific, traumatic, ghastly war then yet seen, claiming millions of lives and casting such a dark shadow over people's minds that we have never recovered. And if there had been no First World War, maybe there would have been no Second World War, since Hitler's rise in Germany was a direct consequence of the reparations from the first war, and the lives of tens of millions of people around the world would have been saved. There might have been no Holocaust ...

Of course, the train of subsequent events would be so tangled, so infinitely varied in possibilities that it's impossible to even speculate on the effect of such an intervention. Maybe the story of the world, released from such a terrible fate, would have been of incredible joy and wonder as lives and attitudes improved. Or maybe it would have turned to one of even greater calamity. And maybe, too, just as in chaos theory the flapping of a butterfly's wings in Brazil can set off a tornado in Texas, so even a small intervention in history, rather than something as marked as averting Franz Ferdinand's assassination, might have had massive consequences for the world's story.

But even if the time machine I am supplied with only allows me to witness things rather than intervene, I surely should try to learn something that I might bring back to help the world now. Of course, the chances are that on my return my discoveries would be treated as the ravings of a fantasist. But what if I were able to convince people of what I'd seen? Again, it's impossible to know, since the chances are that I might learn something just as important from some small, surprising moment than one of history's Big Events. As an agnostic, I can imagine the impact on my life personally – and maybe the future world if I could acquire convincing evidence – of going back and discovering, say, that the Biblical story of Christ was literally true. Of course, if it turned out to be not true at all, the time trip would have been wasted.

So again, I think perhaps I should just go where the ride takes me …

Are you cool? *(Philosophy, Politics and Economics, Oxford)*

It's just possible this question is about my physical comfort on a hot day. If so, I could say 'yes' with a fair degree of confidence and precision. In fact, I know just how cool I am to within a few tenths of a degree (36.8°C), because like all mammals we humans have a remarkably good feedback mechanism for thermoregulation that ensures that our body temperature remains pretty much steady. Indeed, we humans are probably the coolest of all mammals because we have especially good mechanisms for keeping cool. Unlike other mammals, we have no fur, and can lose heat by sweating profusely. Only horses sweat as much, and horses don't walk upright so more of their body is exposed to the heat of the sun. Interestingly, though, with a drop in body temperature of less than a degree I'd turn from cool to cold. A drop of much more than a degree and I'd go from cold to hypothermia, with my skin turning blue, my extremities numb and my whole body shivering in a futile attempt to keep warm …

Of course, this question is probably meant to be about metaphorical cool, not body cool! In the last decade, at least, 'cool' has become such a ubiquitous word for all things good among the younger generation that it's actually no longer cool. Cool is too ordinary, too much used by all kinds of people to quite live up to its name. The concept of cool will surely survive, though. It's an old idea – the idea of ironic, apparently effortlessly superior detachment from the mainstream. Aristotle identified it in his *Nicomachean Ethics*. The Italian Renaissance style guru Baldassare Castiglione in his guide for courtiers talked about *sprezzatura* – an aristocratic nonchalance and distance which disguises all traces of effort, perfectly characterised in Leonardo da Vinci's *Mona Lisa*. And at the bottom of the heap there have always been those celebrated for their ironic and rebellious wit in dealing with their oppressed status.

But what we call 'cool' today probably comes originally from the black jazz scene of the American 1930s and 40s, where windows in smoke-choked clubs were left open on even the coldest nights, leading to the term 'cool jazz' for the seductive style of music played there. The languid detachment of jazz 'cool', though, was completely transformed by the rebellious rise of hip-hop and rap culture. That turned cool into something so aggressive and powerful – not just style but attitude – that it spread far beyond its black roots into youth culture as a whole.

That attitude of cool was an essential way for young black men, pushed to the fringes of society, to give themselves some pride and self-respect. But as it has spread wider, the nature of cool has changed. In one direction, it has just become an ordinary, harmless, friendly word of affirmation and praise, but in another it has acquired a far more divisive image. It has become a badge for the cool inside crowd among the young (and the would-be young) – those in the know, informed, stylish, fashionable, dismissive – that separates them from the non-cool outsiders – ill-informed, lacking in style, the sheeplike 'losers'. It's often a means, now, of bullying psychologically (and sometimes physically) those who don't fit in. And more depressing still, it's become a means for advertisers to create and exploit aspirational markets. What an irony that the once rebellious nature of 'cool' is often now linked with expensive, exclusive style affordable only to the ultra-rich!

It's this oppressive, aggressive and exclusive side to cool that makes me declare ardently, no I'm not cool. I rebel against the notion of a standard or style or attitude that oppresses those who don't fit in – that excludes and diminishes the vulnerable, the shy, the uninformed and the unconfident. I rebel, too, against the dominance of a set of values which seems so geared towards the superficial and ephemeral. And I rebel against the idea of being cool if it means being detached, distant, uninvolved, dismissive, unresponsive, lacking in emotional honesty – in fact, lacking in all the things that make the world a happier, more sympathetic place.

Ultimately, though, I suspect that whatever I care to think about it, many others wouldn't hesitate to confirm that I'm not remotely cool in any way! I possess none of the attributes that would make me cool, I guess, such as a sense of style, insider knowledge of trends, nonchalance, calm assertiveness and sexual swagger. Yet nor can I say I'm driven by fiery hot-blooded Latin passion. So perhaps I would have to say I'm not cool but tepid …

If there was an omnipotent god, would he be able to create a stone that he couldn't lift? (Classics, Oxford)

This is an ancient question asked by theologists and philosophers to throw into doubt assumptions about God. It's called the stone paradox. It's intended to suggest that God cannot logically be all-powerful – and so probably doesn't exist. The argument goes that either God can create a stone which he cannot lift, or he can't. If he can create this stone, then he can't move the stone, in which case he's not omnipotent. If he can't create the stone, then he can't be omnipotent either because there's something he can't do. Amazingly, theologists and philosophers have been debating this question for hundreds of years, trying to work out what a stone that could not be moved even by an omnipotent being could possibly be like – what it would weigh, what would stop it moving, and so on.

Yet actually it's not really a paradox, because it's simply a question of using mutually exclusive terms. There simply cannot be a stone that cannot be moved by an omnipotent being. It would be the equivalent of a square circle, a married bachelor, a sunny night or a wet desert. So the question is pointless. An omnipotent god cannot create a stone that he cannot lift, but that doesn't mean he is not omnipotent. It's just false logic.

Of course, many theologists would say that God is beyond logic anyway. So in answer to the question, 'Can

God create a stone he cannot lift?' the answer is 'Yes, and he can lift it'. His powers are said to be miraculous beyond human understanding. That's how he created the universe from nothing and could, if he wanted, make 2 + 2 equal 5. QED.

In some ways, though, this leads on to fundamental questions that continue to intrigue yet remain impossible to answer, and that appear to be genuine paradoxes. What was there before the beginning of time, for instance? What is beyond the universe, if the universe is everything there is? Cosmologists now say they believe the universe is finite. But how can a universe, which by definition includes everything, be finite? How can the limitless be limited? How can eternity start and end? It's asking questions like these that has, ironically, turned some cosmologists to belief in God, because it seems there are things that it's genuinely impossible for the human mind to comprehend.

Should someone sell their kidney?

(Medicine, Cambridge)

Ever since organ transplants first became common in the 1960s, there has been a problem sourcing suitable donor organs. An estimated 170,000 people are on the waiting list for kidneys in the USA and Europe, and each year another 5,000 join the queue. Most kidneys for transplant come from dead donors, but since people can usually survive with just one of their kidneys, they can also come from living donors – about 1 in 10 in the UK do and 1 in 4 in the USA. Kidneys from living donors are generally in better condition, and there is a better chance of finding a good match, especially among relatives. Taking a kidney from a living donor also avoids the horrible unpredictability of waiting for someone with a compatible kidney to be killed accidentally or die quickly without damage to the organ.

The problem is, of course, that not everyone has a generous relative sitting by, which is why desperate kidney sufferers in the world's richer countries may look for a donor in the developing world. And with kidneys fetching well over $5,000, many poor people in countries like Pakistan and Colombia have been tempted to sell one of their kidneys. Most governments try to stop the trade in organs, but kidney sufferers in rich countries are desperate for health, and people in poor countries are desperate for money, so the trade continues on the black market, even where it isn't allowed legally. At least 6,000 kidneys are traded around the world each year. In Pakistan, there are many villages where more than two out of five people have just a single kidney.

Those who partake in the trade justify it like this. The kidney sufferer is very ill, and if someone else can help them by donating a kidney, why shouldn't they? And if the kidney sufferer is rich and the donor very poor, why shouldn't they show their gratitude with a generous cash payment? That way, two people benefit: the recipient who gets his new kidney and a new lease of life, and the donor who gets a cash payment that transforms his life and maybe that of his entire family. According to David Holcberg of the Ayn Rand centre, it's a matter of self-determination: 'The right to buy an organ is part of your right to life. The right to life is the right to take all actions a rational being requires to sustain his life. This right becomes meaningless when the law forbids you to buy a kidney or liver that would preserve your life.' Holcberg argues that poor people 'do have the capacity to reason'.

But, of course, it isn't as simple as that. Donating a kidney is not an everyday, harmless procedure like selling a chair. Undergoing the operation to remove the kidney can be traumatic, and very occasionally fatal. Sometimes a botched operation carried out in secret can leave the donor desperately ill. Even if the operation goes smoothly, the donor may survive perfectly well on one kidney, but is left with no back-up. Many poor fishermen in southern India who sold a kidney in the wake of the 2004 tsunami now bitterly regret it.

The question does not address whether someone should buy an organ, but it's a question worth answering – and the answer, to my mind, has to be 'no'. Of course, it's wonderful if a kidney is donated freely and generously, but as soon as money is involved, the pressure of payment becomes the dominant issue. You cannot avoid the possibility that you are exploiting someone's desperation – and risking their health. It's no coincidence that paid donors cannot be found in the rich countries of the world; they can be found only in poor countries where people often feel they have no choice and would willingly sacrifice their health for the sake of a better life for them or their families. As William Saletan wrote in *Slate* magazine in 2007, the donor will be 'a fisherman or an out-of-work laborer who needs cash and can't find another way to get it. The middlemen will open him up, take his kidney, pay him a fraction of the proceeds, and abandon him, because follow-up care is just another expense. If he recovers well enough to keep working, he'll be lucky.'

Interestingly, though, the question comes at the issue from the donor's point of view and asks should the donor sell a kidney. Here the answer isn't so clear. As a (comparatively!) rich Westerner, of course I can't say the donor should sell, and yet nor can I disapprove of the donor who chooses to sell, even at risk to his or her health. I would never want anyone put in the position where they are tempted to sell a kidney, but I can entirely understand how someone would willingly accept the suffering and risk to give themselves or their family a better life. Indeed, maybe I would even admire their courage, while condemning the terrible inequalities that drove them to it. If the question was 'would I?' and I could transform the lives of my friends and family by acting as a donor, I might hesitatingly say 'yes' and prepare myself to live with the consequences. The hesitation would be that by putting myself at risk I could increase, not reduce, my family's hardships, and that might be enough to stop me. But to the question 'should someone?' the answer must clearly be 'no' – because that is a question only the donor can decide, and no one else. It's a hard choice; there is no 'should' about it.

Is it moral to hook up a psychopath (whose only pleasure is killing) to a reality-simulating machine so that he can believe he is in the real world and kill as much as he likes? *(Philosophy, Cambridge)*

It's certainly a gruesome, distasteful idea and reminiscent of some low-budget horror film – with the terrible twist being that the simulated killing turns real. And the idea of allowing a psychopath to indulge in this ghastliest of fantasies seems deeply shocking. But however much the idea provokes outrage, it is a valid question.

Of course, if the situation posed were to arise, the chances are it would be in a hospital where the psychopath was already being treated for his affliction. In this case, it would be our moral duty to ensure his well-being. It's hard to imagine how the killing machine could be anything but a retrograde step in his treatment. So unless there was strong evidence to the contrary, allowing him to indulge in simulated killing would be neglecting our duty of care.

If, however, someone were to demonstrate strong evidence that playing the killing machine actually helps in the psychopath's treatment, then it would be entirely moral to hook him up. But should we hook him up against his will? A similar moral question arises over chemical castration or libido-diminishing treatments for dangerous paedophiles, which may increase their chances of living freely without posing a threat to children. Most liberally-minded people would agree that we should never forcibly castrate paedophiles. What we can do at most is to allow them to make that decision themselves – and we'd have to consider carefully the way we provided advice and assistance.

In the same way, it would be moral to hook the psychopath up to the machine only if he actually agrees to it. But we cannot morally force him to, even if we have powerful evidence that it helps; we can only try to persuade him. The same is true of all patients being treated for mental health in hospitals; the treatment must be with their consent. Only if they are genuinely incapable of making an informed decision should any treatment be carried out without their consent, and even then only with the informed consent of those charged with their care. It doesn't matter what we think. Mental patients, even psychopaths, have a right to decide for themselves, as long as they are capable of making a decision and as long as their decision doesn't harm anyone else.

Interestingly, though, while we might reel in disgust from the idea of the killing machine, a crime in the mind is actually very different from a real crime. We all have fleeting thoughts and fantasies about doing something that could be criminal. When angry we might momentarily have had a vision of burning the school down or killing the boss. But most of us know even at the moment we think it that we would never really do it. We may not be able to control all our thoughts and fantasies, but we can control our actions. And while we might personally fight against 'evil' thoughts, and others might fight to stop us having them, society cannot and should not police our thoughts, only our actions.

So if the psychopath's game with a cyber killing machine harmed no one, then we would not necessarily have the right to interfere in a hypothetical situation in which he has access to the machine. There is no reason why we should actually help him, of course, either by providing him with the machine or hooking him up. And if he is in prison, the prison authorities would be entirely right to refuse to provide a machine and to hook him up if they chose to. Interestingly, though, prison authorities do allow prisoners access to computer games in which they can commit virtual, often quite violent crimes. Whether this is wise or not is open to question, but it's certainly not a problem of morality.

Should obese people have free NHS treatment? *(Social and Political Sciences, Cambridge)*

Of course they should. The NHS is intended to provide free treatment for all. The question may be intended to arouse indignation in a diminishing majority of thin people. Obesity is a major risk factor in some illnesses, such as heart disease, and some people are obese because they choose to overeat. It could therefore be implied that their illness could be, in part, self-inflicted and therefore shouldn't be treated free. However, there are almost no grounds on which to make a good case. In no illness, for instance, is there a direct cause-and-effect link with obesity, and only in some is it a major risk factor. Moreover, many of the health problems that obese people suffer are nothing whatsoever to do with their weight.

More importantly, even if every illness an obese person suffered could, in fact, be shown to be directly caused by their weight, it would be completely unreasonable to refuse them free treatment. We cannot be sure that they chose to be obese (very few people do!). Yet even if they did, we must acknowledge that people also persist in indulging in dangerous activities such as riding motorbikes, smoking, drinking, working on oil rigs and down coal mines – all of which put their health at risk. Yet the NHS quite rightly treats all these people free, even if there is a direct cause and effect between their health problem and their lifestyle. The ethos is for the NHS to treat all people who need treatment without charge, not treat them according to their lifestyle.

That said, the NHS does have finite resources and so, to some extent, has to distribute treatment according to need. That means, of course, that urgent, life-threatening or severe illnesses must always get priority. Doctors must also decide how much of their resources they are going to put into treating each case. Some patients will not necessarily be prescribed a drug that would alleviate their condition simply because it is very expensive for the benefits it produces, and money and resources are deemed better spent elsewhere. Such decisions about priority are being made all the time and provoke a great deal of questioning and controversy.

It's in this light that questions such as the one about not treating obese people must be seen. Doctors are within their rights to refuse to treat doggedly persistent smokers for smoking-related ailments and recalcitrant alcoholics for alcohol-related illnesses. The cause-and-effect relationship between obesity and illness is not quite so clear-cut. Nevertheless, levels of obesity are steadily growing in the UK, and the health problems it creates are imposing a growing burden on the NHS. One in four people in the UK were obese in 2007, and the proportion is swelling all the time, especially amongst young people. Health experts talk of an obesity time bomb, with the associated health problems likely to put massive pressure on resources in the future. This is why the government is under pressure to launch as powerful a public information campaign against obesity as past governments have against smoking. Refusing to treat obese people on the NHS, however, will solve nothing.

Why did they used to make the mill chimneys so tall? (Engineering, Cambridge)

Actually most chimneys are tall; mill chimneys were just taller. Chimneys need to be tall for two reasons. The first is to vent smoke high up into the air where it can be carried away and dispersed by the wind. The second is to provide a good updraft for the fire, and this is probably what really mattered for the mill owners of the Industrial Revolution, who I suspect weren't that worried about pollution as they created the dark, satanic mills that filled the skies with black smoke in Blake's bleak vision. The mills of the early Industrial Revolution were of course driven by steam power, and the tall chimneys provided the powerful up-current make the fire burn intensely enough to create the steam to drive all the mill's machines.

Tall chimneys provide a good updraft because of the pressure difference between the inside of the chimney and the outside. The heat of the fire makes the fumes or 'flue gases' expand and become less dense and so rise up the chimney. The result is that the flue gases filling the chimney are at a much lower pressure than the outside air. The pressure difference draws air into the fire through a vent near the base of the chimney and so makes the fire burn more fiercely. On the whole, the taller the chimney, the more pronounced this effect, known as the stack effect, is. Build a tall chimney and you get a big pressure difference, a strong updraft and a roaring fire hot enough to generate the steam to drive a lot of heavy machines.

Build your chimney too tall, however, and the flue gases cool too much by the time they reach the top of the chimney and the effect is diminished. So the height of the chimney needed to match the needs of the mill's steam engine, which is why the chimneys at the onset of the Industrial Revolution were shorter than those later on. As the machines got bigger and the steam engines got more powerful towards the mid-nineteenth century, so the chimneys soared to amazing heights. (I suspect that the updraft in a tall chimney is also enhanced by the stronger, more reliable winds that blow over the chimney top far above the ground. Tall chimneys may also be less affected by the temperature inversions that sometimes virtually stop smoke rising in certain atmospheric conditions.)

The tallest mill chimney of all was the Port Dundas Townsend chimney in Glasgow, built in 1859, which at 138.4 metres (454 feet) was the tallest man-made structure in the world until outstripped by the Eiffel Tower in 1889. But there were many other mill chimneys in mid-Victorian times that towered well over 100 metres. As steam engines gave way to other kinds of power, however, mill chimneys gradually became redundant, and the tallest. stacks belonged to steel smelters and power stations. Once the dark, smoky skies of industrial regions were filled with the mill chimneys that rose up like forests of gaunt, leafless trees across the landscape. Now only a few survive – haunting reminders of the origins of the modern urban world.

Why can't you light a candle in a spaceship? *(Physics, Oxford)*

Well, actually you can light a candle in a spaceship. It would just be a very, very foolish thing to do if it was a conventional wax candle. Out in space, of course, there is no air, so spaceships must create their own oxygen-containing internal atmosphere for the astronauts to breathe. If the candle burns oxygen faster than the spaceship's systems can replenish it, the astronauts would soon die of oxygen starvation. Even if the ship's oxygen supply could keep pace with candle's oxygen consumption, it would dramatically shorten the mission.

Worse still, if the spaceship's atmosphere is oxygen-rich, lighting a candle could start an inferno. The dangers of this were tragically illustrated in 1967 when three astronauts in America's Apollo 1 space capsule lost their lives. Earth's atmosphere is about 21 per cent oxygen and 78 per cent nitrogen, but in the lower pressures encountered in space, an atmosphere this rich in nitrogen would have given early astronauts the bends. The bends, otherwise known as decompression sickness, plagues scuba divers and occurs when nitrogen bubbles form in the blood, which can lead to paralysis and even death. So the capsule was filled with pure oxygen. Unfortunately, this proved fatal, because without the nitrogen to slow reactions down, oxygen is highly combustible. So when a spark started a fire, it engulfed the entire capsule in a ball of fire in less than a minute.

On later Apollo missions, the astronauts wore oxygen-filled spacesuits for lift-off, while the cabin was filled with a safer mix of 60 per cent oxygen and 40 per cent nitrogen. Only once the spacecraft was up in space and past the dangerous take-off stage was the nitrogen vented and the cabin atmosphere turned to pure oxygen, allowing the astronauts to take off their helmets. It was still a high-risk strategy, and even a brief electrical spark could have brought disaster, let alone a candle.

Now space missions and orbiting space stations use a mixture of oxygen and nitrogen similar to earth's atmosphere, and the spaceship's atmosphere is kept pressurised at a similar pressure too, to avoid the problem of the bends. So lighting a candle would not be quite so instantly catastrophic, but it would still consume vital oxygen at a terrifying rate. Short space missions like the American space shuttles and the Russian Buran are brief enough for the oxygen to be supplied entirely from tanks of liquid oxygen.

Space stations, however, must generate their own oxygen supply and recycle as much as possible. Blowers continually circulate air through the spaceship and into ducts where impurities are removed. A bed of charcoal soaks up smells. Fine filters trap floating particles. Cold plates like refrigerator coils condense moisture from the astronauts' breath and feed the water into a tank. Carbon dioxide from the astronauts' exhalations is more of a problem, and is usually absorbed in canisters of lithium hydroxide, then simply vented into space.

In the Russian Elektron and American Oxygen Generation systems, new oxygen is created from water collected from the cold plates and from urine and waste washing. The water is split into hydrogen and oxygen by electrolysis, and the oxygen is supplied to the cabin crew, while the hydrogen is vented into space or made to react with waste carbon dioxide to produce methane and water, which can be used for washing, or for making more oxygen. Neither of these systems, though, has yet proved completely reliable, so keeping astronauts supplied with oxygen on long missions remains a problem. So you might be able to burn a candle in the space station, but it would prove a constant drain on the oxygen-generating systems because, unlike human breathing, it consumes oxygen as it burns without producing much water for recycling.

There is a final twist to this question, because the International Space Station, like Mir before it, carries an emergency oxygen supply in the form of 'oxygen candles'.

Made of lithium or sodium perchlorate, these are flares that burn slowly to produce lithium or sodium chloride, iron oxide and oxygen. The candles burn for about six hours, and the International Space Station has 350 of them, enough to keep three people breathing for three months. So you can burn an oxygen candle in a spacecraft, and it could save your life! Even oxygen candles are not entirely safe, though. One burned out of control on Mir in 1997. Fortunately, no one was injured, although the space station was damaged. More tragically, it's thought that an explosion of one of these candles caused the death of two sailors aboard the nuclear submarine HMS *Tireless* beneath the Arctic in 2007.

If I could fold this paper an infinite number of times, how many times must I fold it to reach the moon?

(Physics and Philosophy, Oxford)

The answer is about 43. You can work this out very roughly, knowing that the distance to the moon is a little less than 400,000 km and that a thin sheet of paper is about 0.1 mm, or 0.000001 km. You could double 0.000001 until you reach approximately 400,000 or halve 400,000 until you reach roughly 0.000001. The number of folds involved is actually surprisingly small because the thickness of the paper increases exponentially, doubling the thickness increase with each fold. I would take a little while to work this out mentally, without the aid of a calculator, but I just happen to know that it takes 51 folds to reach the sun from the earth,[*] and knowing that the moon is 400 times nearer than the sun, I can work out fairly instantly that it takes eight fewer folds to reach the moon. If you didn't know, you'd simply have to work the answer out slightly more laboriously.

Folding paper has actually been the subject of serious mathematical analysis for over half a century. Some of the interest, naturally enough, has come from those masters of paper-folding, the Japanese, and the basic mathematical principles or axioms for folding, covering multi-directional origami folds as well as simple doubling, were established by Japanese mathematician Koshiro Hatori in 2001, based on the work of Italian-Japanese mathematician Humiaki Huzita.

Because of the exponential increase in thickness with each fold, it was widely believed that the maximum number of doubling folds possible in practice was seven or eight. Then in January 2002, American high school student Britney Gallivan proved this wrong in a project she did to earn an extra maths credit. First she managed to fold thin gold foil twelve times, and then, when some people objected that this wasn't paper, succeeded in making the same number of folds in paper. Britney went on to devise

---

[*] 51 folds of 0.1 mm-thick paper would produce a wad 2.26 × 1011 metres thick, which is about the distance to the sun.

a formula for calculating the length of paper you need to achieve a certain number of folds (t is the thickness of the paper, n is the number of folds and L is the length):

$$L = \frac{\pi \cdot t}{6} \cdot (2^n + 4)(2^n - 1)$$

Using this formula, Britney showed that you could get further by folding lengthways, but that twelve was pretty much the practical limit for folding paper. So it would be impossible to get more than a metre or so off the ground in practice, let alone all the way to the moon.

Can history stop the next war?

(History, Cambridge)

If the question was '*Will* history stop the next war?', the answer must be almost certainly not. There are wars being fought all over the world right now, and almost all of them have their roots in historical issues. Some of the historical issues are in the recent past; some are fuelled by ancient, yet still burning resentments; some are a mix of both. The conflict between Israel and Arab Palestine, for instance, finds its origins both in ancient tribal and religious differences and in the more recent nature of the division of Palestine in the wake of the Second World War. The war in the Congo stems partly from the legacy of European colonialism. And it's highly likely that historical issues will play a key role in whatever war starts next, whether it's another skirmish between Georgia and neighbouring Russia, or between North Korea and the South.

However, the question asks 'can' history stop the next war*; in other words, might lessons learned from history reduce the chances of a war starting? It seems logical that they might. Surely people learn from their mistakes? The pessimist would say that there is no evidence that they do. If people did learn from history that war is a 'bad thing', then we would surely have seen the frequency and severity of wars decline throughout history as their appalling costs became clear. Yet the last hundred years have seen the most devastating wars of all time – and never a moment without conflict somewhere in the world. In some ways, you could say that the lesson people actually seem to have taken from history, despite what our moral side would like, is that war is not such a bad thing, or at least that it's not so bad that it must be avoided in future. The costs seem never to

---

* One of the interesting things about the Oxbridge questions is that they can be ambiguous, and often the key to providing a 'clever', original answer is to spot these ambiguities. Here, for instance, 'can' is an ambiguous word choice. The questioner could mean: has history the ability to stop the next war? And of course by itself it cannot; history is simply the story of what happened in the past. However, it's a good bet the questioner is asking if lessons that people learn from history could stop the next war. It seems possible, but again the phrasing of the question implies that it almost certainly won't. The next war is, by definition, a war that must start sometime, however near or far in the future, and it seems unlikely that lessons learned from history would ever stop a war once started.

have been so high that they have ever made embarking on another war inconceivable.

Yet there is a more optimistic way of looking at things. After the horror of the First World War, the victorious nations got together to form the League of Nations with the aim of preventing the outbreak of war in future. Yet they made the mistake of punishing Germany, the nation they held responsible for the war, too severely. The economic hardship and loss of national pride drove the Germans into the embrace of Hitler and took the world into an even more widespread and devastating war. After the Second World War, it seems enough people had learned the lessons of the previous disaster to avoid pressing the defeated Germany too hard. Indeed, the famous Marshall Plan helped to rebuild the German economy and trigger its remarkable post-war drive to prosperity and stability – a prosperity and stability which played a major part in undermining the attractions of communism in the east of Europe, and so helped to bring about the end of the Cold War.

People criticise the ineffectiveness of the United Nations, or its domination by the big nations of the Security Council, and yet the establishment of an international forum where nations can air their grievances before going to war is a lesson learned from history. Of course there have been many wars, large and small, since the Second World War – including the Korean, Vietnamese, Iran–Iraq and Gulf wars – and the UN itself has overseen the initiation of some wars, such as the Kosovan conflict, the Afghan war and the invasion of Iraq.

However, it is entirely plausible to argue that the devastation of the two world wars has at least made the major powers stop to think before reacting to issues with a declaration of war, and may have kept conflicts regional rather than global. The rivalry between the Soviet Union and the USA during the Cold War, for instance, never escalated beyond the regional in a way such a rivalry might have done earlier. And it may be that the experience of the horror of the atomic bomb attacks on Japan in 1945 has been behind the determination of the major powers to avoid nuclear war or even major warfare – though of course the moral drawn by some of the American and Russian military from Hiroshima and Nagasaki was also that nuclear weapons are so powerful that they cannot afford to be without their own 'superior' versions. And here we come to the heart of this question.

History is nothing more than the story of the past, and there are as many interpretations of it as there people telling the story. It is certainly worth studying history to learn, in simplistic terms, from our mistakes, but there is not one single history teaching one clear lesson. The lesson many Germans learned from their defeat in the First World War was not to avoid war in future but to make sure they won the next time. Each of us draws our own lessons from history, and applies them in our own way.

And this leads to another problem raised by this question. Who is learning the lessons? Is it individual people? Is it politicians? Is it generals? Is it nations? And how do they put what they have learned into practice in a world that might fundamentally disagree with them, or simply have an entirely different agenda? Ultimately, then, it's impossible to say if history, or rather lessons learned from history, can stop the next potential war; the responsibility belongs to myriad people and events in the here and now. This is not to say that studying history can teach us nothing. No, history may just provide the vital insights to the right people at the right moment that make it possible to avoid going down the same terrible path to war again. As Machiavelli said, 'Whoever wishes to foresee the future must consult the past; for human events ever resemble those of preceding times. This arises from the fact that they are produced by men who ever have been, and ever shall be, animated by the same passions, and thus they necessarily have the same results.'

Where does honesty fit into law?

(Law, Cambridge)

Lawyers have so long been lampooned for their slipperiness and skill at exploiting legal niceties regardless of the truth that it's tempting to say 'nowhere'. Crooked or devious lawyers have been the stuff of stories for centuries.

In the words of the eighteenth-century English poet and dramatist John Gay:

I know you lawyers can with ease
Twist words and meanings as you please;
That language, by your skill made pliant,
Will bend to favour every client.

And of course there is an element of truth in this. Lawyers are often employed by clients to find a way to use the law to protect their interests, not to find the honest course. Viewed in this cynical way, a lawyer's task is to negotiate a path through the thickets of legal restrictions, not to uphold the truth, or even ensure justice. A lawyer might, for instance, be employed to locate a loophole in the law that allows a client to get away with what, to an honest man, looks a lot like robbery.

Indeed, one way of looking at the law would be as a programme for society, providing automatic checks, controls and guidelines to keep society running smoothly and ensure good behaviour – or rather, behaviour that causes no conflict. Like a computer program, the law viewed this way is blind, and honesty becomes irrelevant. All that matters is compliance with the law, and lawyers are simply skilled operators of the program.

But this sci-fi Orwellian view of law, in which individuals are reduced to bit parts, is actually very different from the messy reality in which honesty does and must have a role. It's no accident that the very first thing a witness is asked when he or she steps into the witness box at a trial is the oath to tell 'the truth, the whole truth and nothing but the truth'. This need for honesty is right at the heart of the law.

Of course, nearly all of us are dishonest in some way from time to time. For most, it's no more than telling an occasional white lie. Only for a few is it a major crime. And this is the crux. A system of law is workable only because most people are essentially honest most of the time. If most were essentially *dis*honest, society could probably be kept stable only by military means, and the rule of law would be unworkable. However, if people were entirely honest all the time, laws would be largely unnecessary. All we would probably need were codes with guidelines to help people settle disputes, rather than enforceable laws. The force of law is needed to cope with the, fortunately rare, times when people are dishonest. In theory, it protects the majority of honest people from the minority of dishonest people. Enforceable laws are, of course, a restriction on our freedom but as the philosopher John Locke made clear, we enter a social contract, agreeing to these restrictions on our freedom in return for the protection from others' dishonesty that laws provide.

The legal system would rapidly grind to a halt if we couldn't trust that people are essentially honest most of the time – and the provision 'most of the time' is essential. We don't simply rely on witnesses to tell the truth in court. We rely on officers of the law to be honest, for instance – to tell the truth and not be swayed by undue influence and bribery. If they weren't, the country would no longer be governed by laws but by power networks. And most legal documents carry the rider in 'good faith' – because it's simply impractical to cover every eventuality. Similarly, if crime were too rife, the courts would become clogged and the legal system would break down.

The classic assumption underpinning the criminal justice system, 'innocent until proven guilty' assumes of course that most people are indeed honest. The burden is therefore on the legal system to prove that someone is dishonest, or worse. Imagine how uncomfortable it would be, and how difficult life could become, if officers of the law assumed that all of us were dishonest. That was the problem with the 'sus' laws in the UK that became so unpopular in the early 1980s because of the way they seemed to target racial groups that they were eventually abolished. Recent anti-terrorist legislation provokes the same problems.

But there is a problem with trust that is emerging in the legal systems of the UK and USA in particular. Although a belief in the fundamental honesty of most people is vital to the legal system, a strand of social, political and economic thinking emerged in recent decades that was in some ways opposed to this notion. Ideas such as game theory came to underpin the notion that people are, if not fundamentally dishonest, at least driven ultimately by self-interest to the point where honesty is irrelevant. The classic 'prisoners' dilemma' in game theory* predicts that people must learn to become dishonest, and assume that other people are dishonest, if they are to survive and thrive. Such thinking has bubbled up in many places, from Dawkins' notion of the 'selfish gene', to Mrs Thatcher's infamous comment that 'there is no such thing as society', to Reaganomics, Tony Blair's 'targets' for public sector employees – and most notoriously in the deregulation of the finance system.

But there is a problem for the law with this assumption that people are dishonest. Not only does it create distrust at best, and at worst paranoia, it means that the law begins to lack direction (except when it serves to persecute rather than prosecute). If lawmakers and enforcers start from the assumption that people are dishonest, then there is no guide through the thicket of what makes a good law and what a bad. It becomes hard to judge what is simply

---

* In the famous prisoners' dilemma of game theory, two suspects are arrested and imprisoned separately. With insufficient evidence, the police offer a deal. If either testifies against the other, he will be set free and the betrayed party will get a ten-year sentence. If they both remain silent, they each receive a six-month sentence. And if they each testify against each other, they each get five years. So what should you do if you were one of the prisoners? It would seem that the best 'strategy' is to assume that the other prisoner will betray you. If he does betray you, the worst you get is five years, and if he doesn't, you go free. Many social theorists have gone on to assume that society must run on the same assumptions – that in reality people will make decisions in their own interest with no real reference to honesty. And so, this argument goes, the law must be based on the premise that people are fundamentally dishonest. The interesting thing, though, is that people conform to expectations.

protecting against likely dishonesty of the people and what is actually persecution or, in effect, martial law.

I wonder – though of course, this is sheer kite-flying – if this is one reason why the recent New Labour government in the UK, led by a party which has always been seen as the party of social justice, has sometimes seemed lacking in focus in legislation. I wonder, too, if an assumption that people are dishonest, and a legal system framed as if they are, actually helps to turn them that way ...

What books are bad for you?

(English, Cambridge)

Well, speaking personally, quite a lot of books are bad for me. I suffer from an allergic reaction to the mould spores that billow off any book that's been sitting for a while gathering dust – which is a really positive incentive not to leave them unread for too long!

In the USA, recently, they started to introduce a law, the Consumer Product Safety Improvement Act, saying all books pre-1985 are bad for children, because the inks used to print them contain lead. Some of the pigments used in medieval manuscript books were poisonous, too, such as lead white and vermilion, so no doubt they were bad for you if, like many scribes, you had the habit of licking your brush to bring it to a point. In Umberto Eco's *The Name of the Rose*, some of the monks are poisoned by arsenic on the pages of manuscripts when they wet their fingers to turn the pages. And in Webster's play *The Duchess of Malfi* (1612–13), the Cardinal's mistress Julia dies after kissing a book that has been deliberately poisoned. I'm sure, too, that over time, not a few people have acquired a headache after a clout with a heavy tome, or a bruised toe, and in Forster's *Howard's End*, the character Leonard Bast is killed by a falling bookcase. Indeed, death by falling bookcase seems to be a popular literary device, resonant with ironic symbolism for a victim obsessed by books.

However, maybe we should focus on the verbal content of books, rather than books as weapons. People have often lamented the effect of bad – that is, low-quality – books. Like bad daytime TV, trashy romances and thrillers are said to turn people's minds to mush. People were saying much the same thing 200 years ago. Back in the time of the Napoleonic wars, the older generation in particular shook their heads and rued the effect of the new gothic and romance novels of authors such as Ann Radcliffe and Madame de Staël then so much in vogue with young girls. What these girls needed, they insisted, was a bracing dose of Socrates and Tacitus rather than these lightweight fictions that did nothing but inflame the imagination. And of course such attitudes rubbed off on some of the more high-minded youngsters. In her book on *Women and Gender in 18th-Century Russia*, Wendy Rosslyn quotes an earnest adolescent girl who pompously proclaims that 'novels do not do you any good and only lead you away from really good books'. *Plus ça change*?

Among those indecently inflamed imaginations, of course, were great authors such as Jane Austen and Mary Shelley – not to mention a whole generation of other women whose imaginary worlds and ambitions were so crucially enlarged by reading 'trashy' novels. Just as now we can see the positive side of those early gothic and romantic novels, maybe people will in time see the value of what seems trash now.

Beyond low-quality literature, though, there are throughout history books that have been considered so dangerous that they have been consigned to the bonfire. Indeed, whole libraries such as the Greek library at Alexandria and the House of Wisdom in Baghdad have been consigned to the flames. For most libertarians, the burning of any book is deplorable. It's not simply that it's a curtailment of free speech, though that is worrying enough, but a book is somehow even more precious, as a distillation of thought, a child of the human mind. That's why the Nazi bookburnings seem a tragedy. So do the Spanish conquistadors' burning of Mayan codices.

And yet, there are some book burnings that most of us would actually condone – such as the police disposal of books of child pornography. As a libertarian, I hesitate to say that it's right to destroy any book, or that categorically any book is harmful, but a book of child pornography probably is, not primarily because the contents are corrupting, though they may be, but because the production of the book involved abuse. Any book that could be produced only by abusing someone would be bad to encounter for any purpose other than to prevent the abuse.

There may be a difference, of course, between books that are 'bad' for me personally and books that may be 'bad' for people in general. Conservatives and reactionaries believe that there are such things as dangerous books; books that are bad for people. The conservative news forum *Human Events* asked sympathetic scholars to come up with a list of what they considered to be the most harmful books of the last two centuries. Not surprisingly, Marx and Engel's *Communist Manifesto* comes top of the list. Also near the top is Hitler's *Mein Kampf,* the thoughts of Chairman Mao and the *Kinsey Reports* on sex. A less obvious inclusion is John Dewey's 1916 *Democracy and Education,* which the authors of the list claimed encouraged a skills- rather than knowledge-and-character-based approach to schooling which 'helped nurture the Clinton generation', and J.M. Keynes' thesis on economics, which they say has saddled the USA with massive public debt. These inclusions begin to show why the notion of 'harmful books' is problematic; who is to say what is harmful and what is not? For others, Dewey and Keynes are enlightened and seminal writers.

Of course, one can argue that without *Mein Kampf* neither the Holocaust nor the Second World War would have happened, or that without the *Communist Manifesto* Russia would never have suffered Stalin's brutal regime. But it's important to distinguish books from their readers. Books can be immensely powerful. The ideas in them can change the way people think. Yet it was the Nazis and Stalin's officers who committed terrible crimes, and not *Mein Kampf* or the *Communist Manifesto* – and of course, the *Manifesto* contained many key ideas that are still relevant and important today, long after Stalin has gone. There is a crucial distinction between the book and its effect – it's crucial because if you talk about a book being harmful rather than its effect you begin to legitimise censorship. Abhorrent ideas need to be challenged by better ones, not banned.

If the questioner was asking what books are bad for me personally, I'd have a different answer. I'd like to think I am clear-headed enough to be able to read books like *Mein Kampf* – I haven't actually read it – without any ill-effects. But maybe there are books that are bad for me personally. In my teenage years, there were books I became so engrossed in that I missed homework – books such as, early on, *The Lord of the Rings* and later, *Bleak House*. And while working as a road sweeper in the vacations, I couldn't help myself stopping every now and then to read the next chapter of *War and Peace* in between sweeps. I'm sure I only escaped the sack because all the other sweepers did much less work than me without any literary distractions. So in the wrong time and wrong place the very best books could be said to be bad for me. Of course, in the long run, I feel my life was so much enriched by reading these books that they were nothing but good.

There have been, too, books which have made me miserable with their bleak storylines, or envious because of the richness and wonder of the characters' lives compared to mine, or bored and depressed by the sheer awfulness of the writing, or simply jealous because of the financial success of their bestselling author. All of these books might be said to be bad for me, too. And yet without most of them I feel my experience of life would be poorer.

What would happen if you drilled through the earth all the way to the other side and then jumped into the hole? *(Engineering, Cambridge)*

The world's deepest man-made hole is the Kola Superdeep Borehole beneath the Kola Peninsula in Russia, which plunges 7.6 miles below the surface. Drilling began in 1970 and went on for 24 years, until it became too hot to continue – and that shows just how hypothetical this question is. This 'superdeep' hole has penetrated less than 0.1 per cent of the way through the earth, yet already has been utterly defeated by heat and pressure.

So to answer this question, we have to assume that magic has allowed this hole to be drilled and for the bore so stay open rather than collapse. If so, how many other elements of magic do we assume? My guess is that we're being asked to forget the likelihood of being fried by the earth's internal heat before falling more than a few miles into the hole, or crushed by the rising air pressure before falling much further (but see below). My guess, too, is that we're being asked to ignore the likelihood of the earth's rotation and motion through space quickly flinging you fatally against the side of the hole – unless it's a very, very wide hole or the hole is at just the right angle. Of course, with luck you'd black out from the speed of the fall a while before you met your demise …

This is actually a popular conundrum that many people have tried to answer. Yet there are so many ifs and buts that each answer is pretty meaningless and my speculations here are no less so.

So for a moment, forget that you're human, and imagine that you're completely indestructible. If the borehole were air-filled, the air would get increasingly dense towards the centre of the earth. It would at first be liquid, probably not that far down into the hole, and then solid, so the hole would be blocked. If you jumped in, you'd fall increasingly fast under the pull of gravity, until you reached normal terminal velocity as the acceleration due to gravity was matched by increasing air resistance. Very soon, though, you'd begin to slow down as the air became increasingly dense. It would be a little like diving into a pool. Your momentum would carry you a certain way down, but then you'd bob back up again and float on the dense air a little way down the hole, as if you'd fallen in a well.

OK, what if, instead, the borehole were a vacuum-tube and the earth were stationary? Well, then, there'd be nothing to stop you accelerating to an astonishing speed as you plunged into the hole. Nothing, that is, except the pull of earth's gravity. As you plunged nearer and nearer the centre of the earth, you'd pass through more and more of the earth's mass which would then begin to hold you back. It's likely that the braking effect of the mass of the earth's gravity that you passed by as you fell would slow you down to a standstill long before you reached the centre of the earth, where the acceleration due to gravity is nought. Your momentum would mean you'd probably overshoot by a little way the point where gravity pulling you down was balanced by gravity holding you back, but you'd soon 'fall' back up to the balance point and overshoot until you started to fall again. Eventually, after oscillating a few times, you'd hover at the balance point. Since the radius of the earth is 4,000 miles, I guess this balance point would be around 1,000 miles down. And there you'd be, hovering in the dark, until someone was kind enough to throw a magic rope down …

Does a Girl Scout have a political agenda? *(Law, Oxford)*

First of all, it's worth asking what a political agenda is. An agenda is simply a list of things to do, but in the context of politics it has come to have a slightly more pejorative meaning. A *political* agenda could simply mean a list of things for a political party to do. More often, though, it's something neither quite spoken nor written down. It may be the general tendency of politics across the spectrum. Or it can be the hidden political aims of an apparently apolitical organisation, and this is what the question is about: do Girl Scouts have aims that can be seen as essentially political, even though they are not officially a political organisation?

Interestingly, the question asks 'Does a Girl Scout …?' rather than 'Do the Girl Scouts …?' which is subtly different, but I'll address the second first. The Girl Scouts are the American version for girls of the raft of youth organisations started by Lord Baden-Powell in the early twentieth century. Their uniform and very traditional value system have often suggested a kind of militarism, especially since Baden-Powell was himself a soldier. Yet Baden-Powell set up the Boy Scouts to get away from the militarism of the Boys' Brigade and the uniform was intended to eliminate differences in social standing. The idea was to develop independence and resourcefulness combined with a strong sense of duty in young people. In retrospect, maybe, the traditional values of scouting have given it the aura of a political movement. But the aim of the Scouts was not to change society or the way it's governed, which must be the aim of a political movement, but rather to mould individuals. It was about self-improvement, not social improvement – and this is still largely so.

When Juliette 'Daisy' Low came back to America to set up the Girl Scouts in 1912 after working with the Girl Guides in the UK, her aim was slightly different. While she wanted to give America 'something for all the girls' just like the Guides, there was a general move afoot in the USA to give women more independence. It was not a movement for political power as such, but it was for social power, and it was attached to a liberal, Democratic political agenda. The Girl Scout organisation could be said in some ways to have been created by women who emerged from this movement, and there has always been a sense that despite its espousal of traditional values, the Girl Scout movement had liberal political sympathies. In recent years, right-wing commentators have commented on how speakers at Girl Scout conferences have sometimes had 'radical' political agendas, insinuating that the movement has been tainted by the presence on the platform of 'pro-lesbian, pro-abortion' speakers. But being willing to listen to particular political views – and even being sympathetic to them – would not turn the Girl Scouts into a movement with a political agenda.

It might be argued that the Girl Scouts have a particular set of ideals, a particular code of social behaviour that they want to promote. They believe in community and group identity and support the idea of hierarchies of rank, earned on merit. But it would be stretching a point to say that the organisation has a political agenda – that it has intentions to change the system of government, or even to change society at large. Their aim is to promote these values primarily among their own members, each one of whom joins voluntarily, and if promotion goes beyond the Scouts, it's simply to encourage membership.

There is a superficial similarity to other uniformed youth movements (uniforms and youth and traditional values), like the Hitler Youth and more recently the Bajrang Dal, the youth wing of the fundamentalist Hindu movement in India, both of which had or have obvious political agendas. Yet it would be stretching the notion of a political agenda to suggest the Girl Scout movement has one – which is not to say that some members of the organisation do not have political agendas which they join the movement to promote, and use the Girl Scouts to promote.

This brings us on to the question: 'Does a Girl Scout …?' It may well be that many Girl Scouts do have a political agenda, but when it comes to the average Girl Scout, I would say almost certainly not. It's true that when she joins the Scouts, she embraces certain values. She must promise:

> On my honor, I will try:
> To serve God* and my country,
> To help people at all times,
> And to live by the Girl Scout Law.

---

* Since the 1990s, the inclusion of God has been optional.

The Girl Scout law says: 'I will do my best to be: honest and fair, friendly and helpful, considerate and caring, courageous and strong, and responsible for what I say and do, and to respect myself and others, respect authority, use resources wisely, make the world a better place, and be a sister to every Girl Scout.'

By embracing these views she signs up to a particular way of looking at society and accepts it. But this does not mean she has a political agenda. It's not her purpose to change the system of government or the nature of society as a whole. Indeed, I'm sure most Girl Scouts join with no political intentions at all. They join for the fun activities, to feel a sense of belonging and to make friends. So, on an individual level, the *average* Girl Scout probably does not have a political agenda, even though there may be many Girl Scouts who do.

What does it mean to be happy?

(Philosophy and Modern Languages, Oxford)

If there's one thing that most people agree about, it's that they want to be happy. But it's surprisingly hard to pin down just what happiness is. It can be both a brief moment of pleasure and a lasting sense of well-being – of feeling good, in all senses of the word. Oddly enough, although it's so universally wanted, most of us very rarely say that we are happy unless specifically asked – and even then it tends to make us stop and think a while, 'Am I happy?' That, of course, does not mean at all that we are not happy – just that we do not think about it when we are. In some ways, when we are happy, we no longer need to strive for it and so cease to be aware of it. The great Victorian philosopher John Stuart Mill wrote, 'Ask yourself whether you are happy, and you cease to be so'.

In an article in the *New Internationalist* in 2006, clinical psychologist John F. Schumaker argued that in this consumer age, we have become obsessed with the search for happiness, citing the avalanche of self-help books, articles, TV programmes, websites, courses and so on that guide us towards the nirvana of personal bliss. We're all after those feel-good moments, those blissed-out moments of joy because 'we're worth it'. And yet somehow, the harder we search, the harder we find it to achieve. As Søren Kierkegaard wrote, 'Most men pursue pleasure with such breathless haste that they hurry past it'.

When it comes to personal satisfaction, most people say they are 'happy' in answer to surveys – and yet seem to acknowledge that there's something missing. Apparently, we only laugh a third as often as we did 50 years ago, and we make love more infrequently and enjoy it less, despite the sexual revolution which has removed the sense of guilt and unleashed a flood of sexual imagery in the media. And in Western society, where material pleasures, from good food to comfortable homes and exciting foreign travel, are more freely available than ever before, most people seem to be less happy than ever before. There is a depression epidemic and in the Western world a huge proportion of people believe they are psychologically ill-adjusted.

There is a nagging sense that the old saw 'they were poor but they were happy' has some truth in it. At the back of our minds is the feeling that happiness is not really about all the material pleasures the consumer society can bring, despite all the effort we put into achieving them. Some feel that we have been led astray by this search for happiness. 'America', the author John Updike wrote balefully, 'is a vast conspiracy to make you happy', while J.D. Salinger admitted: 'I'm a kind of paranoiac in reverse. I suspect people are plotting to make one happy.'

It might be true indeed that happiness won't come to those who look for it. Schumaker describes how a few decades ago, the small Himalayan nation of Ladakh was one of the most joyous nations on earth. 'Their culture generated mutual respect, community-mindedness, an eagerness to share, reverence for nature, thankfulness and love of life. Their value system bred tenderness, empathy, politeness, spiritual awareness and environmental conservation.' And then in 1980 it all changed as the country was hit by consumer capitalism. Ladakh's new Development Commissioner announced: 'If Ladakh is ever going to be developed, we have to figure out how to make these people more greedy.' They succeeded and the people of Ladakh now experience widespread crime, family breakdown, depression, pollution and deprivation.

Of course, none of this should be a surprise. Over 2,500 years ago, the Greek philosophers debated what it means to be happy and very few came down on the side of hedonism and simple material pleasures. Democritus argued that the supreme goal in life was being cheerful, but a life of pleasure got few other supporters. Epicurus is often misunderstood as the ultimate hedonist – his live-for-pleasure theories badly characterised in the phrase 'Eat! Drink! For tomorrow we die!' But what Epicurus argued was not for chasing after each and every immediate thrill, but rationally ordering your life to achieve the maximum pleasure in the long term. A life lived like that, he argued, would be a happy, virtuous life.

Most of the Greek thinkers, however, were what were called Eudaimons. Eudaimon is a word that cannot easily be translated but it means something like 'well-spirited'. It's about a sense of well-being, of a life of excellence, of being blessed by good fortune. It was, according to Aristotle, about the good life in all senses of the word – a life that was materially pleasant and blessed with good things including a loving family and beauty, successful in terms of accomplishments, and morally virtuous. It is in some ways about having a good soul or achieving what Thomas Aquinas later called 'blessed happiness'. It's perhaps no coincidence that the word happy originally meant 'lucky'.

If I think of the moments in life that I remember most fondly – and so must be the moments of greatest happiness – I think I would have to agree with Aristotle. It's not experiences of material pleasures alone that I cherish, but times when I was surrounded by the love of friends, times when I finished a creative work, times when I was praised by a much-valued voice, times when a kind deed made someone smile, times when I made a great catch at softball, times when I noticed passing beauties such as sun sparkling on water. Of course, there are times of material pleasure in there, too, but all these moments have another, deeper emotional significance as well as sheer physical gratification. I have a feeling that in none of these moments was I actually seeking happiness. Happiness was a by-product. Happiness is an elusive butterfly, the scent of a flower on the wind, caught fleetingly, almost accidentally. Nietzsche, renowned for his gloomy, nihilistic outlook on life, said the key to happiness is to appreciate 'the least, the softest, lightest, a lizard's rustling, a breath, a moment'.

Smith sees Jones walking towards a cliff. Smith knows Jones is blind but doesn't like him, so allows him to walk off the edge. Is this murder? (Law, Cambridge)

Under English law, Smith is not guilty of murder because he did not actually intend to kill Jones. For Smith to be convicted of murder, it's not enough that he foresaw Jones's death clearly and did nothing to prevent it; he has to be shown to have intended it. Since he did not actually push

Jones off the cliff, nor do anything to encourage him to walk towards the cliff, there is no way it could be proved that Smith intended to kill him.

Our initial reaction to this story is that Smith's silence seems shocking. How appalling, deliberately letting a blind man walk off a cliff. Surely he must be guilty! He is not, and if we reframe the story a little, then we begin to see why. What if the reason Smith doesn't like Jones is because Jones is a gang leader who likes to murder innocent people for pleasure – and Jones has just herded up another group of victims? Then Smith begins to look more like a hero than a villain. Of course, if it's Smith who is the murderer and Jones the saint pleading for the hostages to be spared, it all looks very different again. This is why the law has to be framed carefully, and judges and juries must have real, not circumstantial, evidence to convict someone of a crime – and why we must be extremely careful not to imagine motivations.

However, Smith just might be guilty of a serious crime, although it could be hard to prove in court. In English law, that crime is involuntary manslaughter. Involuntary manslaughter is when someone allows the death of someone through extreme carelessness or incompetence or gross negligence. In the USA and other countries, Smith might similarly be guilty of criminally negligent homicide, a less serious crime than first- or second-degree murder. Negligence is not always clearly defined, but in English law it does include omission – omission to do something that would certainly have prevented death. The prosecution, though, might have a tough time showing that Smith really was culpable in this way, because there could be many entirely innocent reasons for his failure to warn Jones. We would probably need witnesses to show exactly how he behaved – and if there were witnesses, why didn't they intervene? CCTV footage might show Smith clearly stepping out of Jones's path, but even that wouldn't necessarily prove he was guilty.

Overall, the chances are that Smith would get away with it. All that would prevent him being a happy man is the terrible burden of guilt that eventually becomes so unbearable that Smith takes his own life by following Jones over the same cliff …

How would you measure the weight of your own head? *(Medicine, Cambridge)*

Not an easy one, since cutting off your head and placing it on the scales would render you incapable of reading the measurements. Keeping your head on your shoulders and resting your head on the scales might not be quite so fatal, but it's unlikely to provide much of a measurement either, since your neck muscles would invariably offer enough support to invalidate the reading. Even an estimate from measuring a similar-sized melon is likely to be more accurate than this!

So the best approach is to try a couple of methods that would give a rough measure and then take an average between them. First you can establish the volume of your entire body by filling a bath enough to entirely immerse yourself. Mark the water level (level 1) and then get in, allowing the water to completely settle down before gently and briefly submerging altogether. Get a friend to mark the water level (level 2), or do it yourself if you can. Get out of the bath and refill it to level 1 to allow for the water you've spilled and dripped out on your body. Now add measured amounts of water until it reaches level 2. The volume of water you added should give you a measure of the volume of your body. It's only a rough measure, so repeat the exercise several times and take the average to reduce the error. (If you have a person-sized drum, this would make a more accurate measure than a bath, since the water level would rise further in the confined space as you got in.)

Now you can measure the volume of your head the same way, immersing your head only up to a certain point – in a bucket rather than a bath to increase the water level movement. A friend would help ensure that this is to the right point. You could actually measure the volume of your body without your head instead, by getting into the bath to measure your body volume, but leaving your head above water.

Finally, weigh your entire body on accurate scales. Now using the ratio of your body volume to your head volume, you can work out the weight of your head from the weight of your whole body.

If you repeated this method several times, you would probably get a reasonable measure of the weight of your head, despite the inaccuracies of your measurements and errors introduced by the air spaces in your head.

A quicker but less accurate method would be to measure the volume of water displaced by your head in a bucket, then convert this figure to a weight of water and add 5 per cent (to allow for the slightly higher specific gravity of your head).

Finally, if you have access to a CT scan, you can get someone to measure both the density and volume of your head and then calculate its weight from that.

What is fate? *(Classics and English, Oxford)*

Fate is the idea that events inevitably turned out as they did because they conformed to a plan set up by some outside, supernatural force.

The idea that the course of one's life is somehow pre-determined is an old one, and crops up in many cultures, as the Arabic *kismet*, for instance, and the Ancient Greek Fates, the trio of goddesses – Clotho, Lachesis and Atropos – who spin webs to control the path of human lives.

Fate is often linked in the imagination with tragedy rather than comedy. We talk about someone's tragic fate, but rarely their comic fate. Fate tends to be presented as cruel and mocking, often playing mischievous games with people's lives as they vainly try to escape their predetermined course – but end up unwittingly pursuing the precise path that leads them to their unhappy end. Thus in the Greek play *Oedipus Rex*, the young Oedipus, learning from the oracles at Delphi of his tragic destiny (fate foretold) to kill his father and marry his mother, flees Corinth and ends up in Thebes, where he unknowingly fulfils his destiny.

The idea of being trapped by fate is a powerful and emotive image, and recurs again and again in literature. It touches the very core of what it means to be human. Those who strive vainly against their lot and fight against fate seem somehow to be heroes, even if they fail. They are those who, like Prometheus stealing the secret of fire, gain their heroic stature by trying to wrest control of the human story away from the gods. They are heroes because they give the human story dignity and pride. They show that even if we fail ever to break the bonds of fate, we are so much more than mere playthings of the supernatural. That's why, however appalling it seems to kill your father and marry your mother, Oedipus is heroic in his anguish. That's why, too, Satan in Milton's *Paradise Lost* is not simply a nasty demon, but a heroic, tragic titan. Nietzsche's superman, the *übermensch*, with his 'will to power' is in some ways the ultimate tragic hero, gaining his status by banishing any idea of gods from the world altogether and courageously staking out a future in a world devoid of fate and devoid of meaning.

Accepting one's fate, on the other hand, can either be seen as Zen-like wisdom – why fight what you cannot fight? – or it can be a way of shelving responsibility. If you commit a crime, you can always blame fate. If you cannot be bothered to take a decision, you can say, 'What's the point?', just like the First World War soldiers who fatalistically sometimes declined to wear uncomfortable helmets, saying that if their number was on a bullet it would get them anyway. In this troubled world, many people turn to astrology for the same reason, and 'it's written in the stars' is the same as saying 'it's fate', or listening to supernatural voices. For most people, fatalism – accepting that your whole life is decided by fate – seems a defeat, a sign of personal weakness, or worse, a corrosive cynicism, like that of Pushkin's Eugene Onegin, Lermontov's Pechorin and even Shakespeare's Hamlet.

Yet philosophers have long had a problem with the concept of fate. It's not so easy to dismiss with logic as it first seems. If you accept that the world runs by cause and effect, if one movement causes a predictable effect, as Newton's Laws of Motion bear out, then the future of the world is mechanically predetermined, right down to the movement of atoms; the events of the past inevitably determine the future. So the future can be changed only by changing the very laws of physics. Since we humans are part of this deterministic universe, then our future, too, must likewise be entirely predetermined. If so, that's not so very different from saying that our lives are controlled by fate, except that it's mechanical laws and not heavenly hands that guide our fate, and our oracles are scientific prediction.

Where, then, is the scope for human free will in this deterministic world? We might believe that we are independently making the decision at this very moment to carry on reading here, or go for a drink, to agree with the ideas expressed or dismiss them as nonsense. Yet is this an illusion? Are we, in fact, trapped in the predetermined course of our lives as surely as Oedipus, blithely thinking that we are heading on our own path, but likewise mechanically fated to end up in our own personal Thebes? Schopenhauer thought we were, suggesting that water might say to itself, 'I could behave as a breaking wave, or a gushing waterfall, or a calm pond, but today I'll choose to be a raindrop', while all the time it's controlled entirely by mechanical forces. Wittgenstein put it even more simply, imagining a leaf in autumn saying, 'Now I'll go this way; now I'll go that'.

Dualists who, like Descartes, think that the mind and body are separate, suggest that we can escape our mechanical fate because the mind is independent of the mechanism of the body and its constraint by physical laws. But then if the mind is independent, and disconnected from the body, how can it affect the mechanism at all? If it's not disconnected, then it cannot be independent. The Greek philosopher Epicurus wondered if the mind could alter the deterministic nature of the universe by making atoms swerve. But just thinking about such improbable mechanisms seems to make the dualist escape from fate less plausible.

So most philosophers are divided between compatibilists, who believe that it's possible to reconcile free will with a mechanical fate, and incompatibilists, who believe that it isn't. The incompatibilists make this kind of argument: the past determines the present and future; you can't control the past; you can't alter how the past determines the future; so you have no control over the present or future. So free will is an illusion. Some philosophers have seen quantum mechanics as a way in which the predictable mechanics of the universe can be subverted. Yet this seems to make us victims of randomness – we are the playthings of luck rather than fate, which seems little better.

To me, though, the impression that I do have some free will and at least some control over the direction of my life is so powerful that I cannot believe it's an illusion. I am convinced in my own mind that I was not fated to write this sentence exactly at this moment … with a slight pause for thought here. And if it *is* an illusion, which I can never know one way or the other, then it still makes sense to behave as if it's not. I will go along with Shakespeare's Cassius, who accepted Caesar's elevation to superstardom far above himself and Brutus with the explanation that if all else is equal:

Men at some time are masters of their fates:
The fault, dear Brutus, is not in our stars,
But in ourselves, that we are underlings.

How would you describe an apple?

(Social and Political Sciences, Cambridge)

'Surely,' said the nineteenth-century American poet and naturalist Henry David Thoreau, 'the apple is the noblest fruit.' And there is no fruit that has acquired such symbolic status and been so overlaid with meaning as this ball of pulp, seeds and skin. From New York City to Macintosh computers, it stands for everything from true knowledge to all that's wholesome, all in a tidy little package. A child is the 'apple of his parents' eyes'. A good kid gone rotten is 'a bad apple'. Apples are the comfort for those sick of love in the 'Song of Solomon'. In fact, apples are pretty much anything you want them to be. And everyone has their own way of describing them.

If you were an artist, you might describe an apple as a roundish fruit typically about the size of a tennis ball (5 to 9 centimetres in diameter). It's not quite round, though, as a closer look would show, for there are indentations on opposite sides – a shallow one at the bottom and a deeper one at the top where the stalk is attached. Some apples, you'd observe, have a glossy, waxy look that glistens with brilliant surface highlights, while others have a rougher, mottled matt texture that is richly and densely coloured. They vary in hue from a whitish green to golden yellow, from russet brown to bright crimson – but the colour is very rarely even. On some shiny green apples, the variations are subtle, with just paler spots and stripes visible here and there, with the occasional small dark spots. On others there are marked differences, especially in ripe apples, with some patches turning bright, warm scarlet and others remaining a sharp green.

A mathematician might come at the description from a different angle. This would be tricky because the shape is variable, and it's a complex shape. It's only very roughly approximate to a sphere. You could say it's an oblate spheroid, since it's slightly flattened at the ends. But that would not allow for the flattening around the sides on many apples, too. And of course, this completely ignores the toroidal indenting at top and bottom. It might be simpler to sum up its shape as apploid. We might even be able to come up with an equation to describe an apploid, by assuming an imaginary, perfectly symmetrical apple. Of course, real apples are never perfectly symmetrical, but our mathematical apploid could be a good model of the average apple.

A botanist might have yet another description: An apple is a pome, a special kind of fruit that grows on *Rosaceae* trees of the Maloid family, which also includes pears, quinces, medlars and rowans. Pomes are distinctive because they are 'accessory' fruits, in which the flesh is not made from the carpels (the fertilised ovary) but grows around them. In an apple, the carpels are the five-pointed star of the core alone, each with its seeds or 'pips'. The shrivelled remains of sepals, style and stamen often form a little complementary five-pointed star at the base of the apple. The apples we eat are cultivars, varieties developed from *Malus domestica*, the cultivated tree taken from the wild *Malus sieversii*, which grows in the mountains of Central Asia.

An organic chemist might describe an apple as an arrangement of cellulose in cells containing water, sugars such as fructose and glucose, mild acids such as malic acid, Vitamin C, minerals and amino acids.

A mythologist could describe an apple in many ways – as the forbidden fruit, the fruit of the tree of knowledge, for instance. It was said to be an apple that the Biblical Eve coaxed Adam to share with her, so that they both learned they were naked and were expelled from the Garden of Eden. Golden apples were the fruit of the Greek Tree of Life in the Garden of the Hesperides, which Hercules had to pluck as one of his Twelve Labours. They were the gifts of Aphrodite, the goddess of love, too. Indeed, pretty much every culture has its own special apple stories.

A greengrocer might describe an apple as 'a lovely eater, really sweet and crisp – delicious' or 'a great cooker, big and juicy'. A cook might add that it's very versatile fruit, which can be used in a huge variety of dishes, including apple pie and apple crumble – not to mention as an accompaniment to pork. A wine merchant could say it's the basic ingredient of cider or calvados. To a harassed parent, an apple might be a healthy way to keep the kids quiet in between meals. For disappointed medieval audiences, a (rotten) apple might be a critical theatre review. William Tell's son might describe an apple as the difference between life and death, or 'dad's psychopathic moment'. To Isaac Newton, it was a matter of some gravity. And for Salvador Dali it could be a nun's posterior or a skull's eye socket …

And finally, listen to the very bad but aptly named romantic poet, Bramley Laxton:

'On the Apple'
(Written at Egremont Russet)
Oh apple, glorious autumn's bounty,
Richest fruit of shortening days,
Come when summer's brightness dwindles
Softly into moistening haze.
In lovely luscious clusters drooping
Your gold and russet globes aglow
Ripe and ready now for plucking –
Can I reach one? Can I? Oh!
Yes, I have you now and swiftly
Bite on flesh so crisp and sweet.
Here's a moment's taste of heaven:
Before the winter, autumn's treat.
Oh orchard pome, gold and delicious,
Let me ask you one thing more:

Please apple fair, you're so appealing,
Come back next year for your encore!

The stage: a platform for opinions or just entertainment – what are your thoughts? *(Education Studies, Cambridge)*

The stage today can be pretty much what the performer wants it to be, yet it's rarely either opinion or entertainment alone. There is quite a difference, for instance, between even the most undiluted piece of 'opinion' theatre and someone giving a political speech in parliament or haranguing passers-by at Speaker's Corner, even though all can be highly theatrical.

A speech seeks to communicate the speaker's ideas directly to listeners. A stage performance seeks to engage the audience's imagination, and help them understand the ideas by living through them in their imagination. This is why, generally, stage performances use characters to tell a story or create a picture, rather than talk to the audience directly. When they do appear to address the audience directly, it's in character or within the imaginary world created for the performance.

It's this creation of an imaginary world that marks out the stage from the direct address of a public speaker. The stage is the arena for the creation of this world, a defined area in which the vision is created – whether it's an actual stage, or simply a subtle imaginary barrier set up by the performers between them and their audience as they wander among them in 'promenade' performances. The stage in essence, then, is a playground for the imagination. Stand-up comedians, singers and musicians all perform upon stages, and all to a lesser or greater extent engage the imagination. What makes the stage in the sense of theatre different is that a story is enacted and a picture embodied.

All stage performances must entertain in the broadest sense. 'Entertain' is a word that came originally from the French *entretenir*, meaning 'hold together' – and that's what theatre seeks to achieve: binding performers and audience together in a communal act of imagination. But of course, by 'just' entertainment, people generally mean something rather less – something that merely makes the audience laugh or smile but rarely makes them think. By contrast, then, 'opinion' theatre would make them think, but maybe not laugh or smile. The juxtaposition, though, is false. Even the crudest jokers are expressing an opinion – and their audience have to think, however shallowly and briefly, in responding. And if the audience doesn't fall asleep, they are entertained in the sense of engagement by even the most undiluted opinion piece.

What really matters is the quality of thought and the richness and worth of the ideas involved, and this may be where modern theatre often loses its way, setting up false opposites between the brash, flashy world of 'sheer entertainment' in West End musicals and the intensely serious world of 'challenging', 'relevant' drama. The irony, then, is that often both end up simply poor – being neither great entertainment nor particularly interesting opinion. (Opinion without knowledge or wisdom is facile and attention-seeking rather than instructive and engaging – and ultimately no more profound or valuable than 'sheer entertainment', besides being much less enjoyable.)

Back in the earliest days of theatre in Ancient Greece, Aristotle in his *Poetics* highlighted the difference between tragedy and comedy, and until recently these were seen as the two kinds of theatre, with countless theatre companies carrying as their trademark the opposite weeping mask of tragedy and the smiling mask of comedy. The essence of comedy was a happy ending, and the audience was intended to enjoy the triumph of a lowly, often mischievous character or outcast. The essence of tragedy was the downfall of a good or noble person through some fatal error, and the audience was intended to feel pity and fear that led them to what Aristotle called 'catharsis' – a purging of these negative emotions. Yet most of the best tragedies are leavened with laughter, because humour helps engage an audience; and many of the best comedies have a darker or sadder side that likewise helps engage the audience's sympathies.

Aristotle traced the origins of both tragedy and comedy to religious rituals, and if the overtly religious element has long since vanished, there remains an element of ritual. Without really thinking about it, as an audience we willingly fall hushed at the beginning of the performance and sit rapt in silence in the dark – a condition that has distant echoes of the ritual trances of primitive religions in which people voyaged in their minds into visions and other worlds.

The Ancient Greeks called dramatists *didaskalos*, which is typically translated as teachers, but a better word might be guides. Dramatists are guides through these visions, and they may be opinionated or entertaining, reflective or passionate, thoughtful or impetuous – in fact, anything they may wish to be. Above all, though, they must, like all the best guides, know their way …

I am an oil baron in the desert and I need to deliver oil to four different towns which happen to lie in a straight line. I must visit each town in turn, returning to my oil tank between each visit. Where should I position my tank to drive the shortest possible distance? Roads are no problem, since I have a sheikh friend who will build me as many roads as I like for free. *(Mathematics, Oxford)*

This appears be intuitively simple. A first guess might be that the tank should be located somewhere on the line between the four towns, at the mid-point between one of the two central towns. Then, if the towns are 1 km apart, this would give two 1-km round trips and two 3-km round trips, a total of 8 km. However, intuition is not always right, and proving that answers like these are correct has led mathematicians into some of the most complex and important of all mathematical problems. Known as optimisation, these are about mathematically finding the best solution to a problem, whether it's the shortest route or the optimum structure.

The shortest distance problem has always fascinated mathematicians, not only because it's an interesting geometrical conundrum, but also because it has clear practical applications. The point we are looking for to locate our oil baron's tank is known as the geometric median, which is the point which minimises the distance to a set of sample points.

Back in the seventeenth century, the great French mathematician Pierre de Fermat posed a similar problem to Evangelista Torricelli, the Italian inventor of the barometer. Fermat's problem was to find the shortest distance from a single point to three sample points. Torricelli ingeniously solved the problem, and the point is now known as the Fermat or the Torricelli point. (German economist and pioneer of globalisation theory Alfred Weber also gets in on the act because of his 1909 thesis on the location of industries, so this question is sometimes called the Fermat-Weber problem.)

Fermat's work gave a solution for three points; the problem of finding the geometric median for four points was actually solved by the brilliant Italian priest and mathematician Giovanni Fagnano dei Toschi around 1750. Fagnano realised that when the fixed points form a convex quadrangle, the geometric median is the intersection point of both diagonals; otherwise it's the fixed point in the triangle formed by the three other fixed points.

Mathematicians now know that there is only one geometric median when the sample points are not in a line. In the special case, when the points are in a line or 'colinear' as in the oil baron's problems, the geometric median is the median. The median is the number that divides the population in half. In the case of the oil baron, it is indeed as we guessed – the midpoint between the two middle towns.

Interestingly, the idea of optimising routes is not simply a geometrical problem. It leads into network theory, a branch of mathematics that has attracted extraordinary interest in recent years. The more people study it, the more relevant it seems as an organising principle to explain how the world really works. Networks crop up everywhere. People network socially. The internet is a network. Transport links form networks. Ecosystems form networks. Computers depend on them. What is really exciting people is how lessons learned in one discipline, such as biology, are feeding into others, such as economics.

The recent banking crisis, for instance, has provoked a number of economic theorists such as Domenico Delli

Gatti and Joseph Stieglitz to try to tease out the problems using network theory, showing how a few banks in a network emerge as connecting hubs with more than their share of links. The problem with this is that when such hubs collapse, they can take down the whole network with them. So the network economists are looking to ecological food webs for remedies, because these have evolved ways of coping with crises better. Species with many links, for instance, are often connected to species with few. An insect may pollinate a wide variety of plants, but each plant may be pollinated by only one or a few insects. That way a catastrophe for even the multi-connected insect affects only a limited part of the network.

As director of network research at the University of Notre Dame, Albert-László Barabási writes: 'The diversity of networks in business and the economy is mind-boggling. There are policy networks, ownership networks, collaboration networks, organizational networks, network marketing – you name it. It would be impossible to integrate these diverse interactions into a single all-encompassing web. Yet no matter what organizational level we look at, the same robust and universal laws that govern nature's webs seem to greet us.'

Think of a painting of a tree. Is the tree real? *(Modern and Medieval Languages, Cambridge)*

The simple and immediate answer to this is that the image is real, but the tree clearly is not, even though it may be a real picture of a real tree. Yet philosophers have always had problems with the notion of reality and our knowledge of it. In commonsense, everyday terms most of us have no problem telling what is real and what is not. Yet when you start to think about trying to define just what reality is, it becomes much more elusive.

Is the test of reality, for instance, a commonsense test – something we see with our own eyes? That seems valid at first, especially since the evidence of our eyes is often backed up with evidence from other senses. But can you be sure it's real? Could it disappear as soon as you stop looking? Could it all be a dream? Or a hologram? How can you tell that you are not just a brain in a vat fed a virtual reality by some mad scientist? And might even memory be an illusion, too – and the world burst into existence a few minutes ago, with all our memories intact? Descartes asserted that the only thing you can be sure of is that you are thinking, an idea summed up in his famous phrase, '*Cogito ergo sum*' – 'I think therefore I am'.

One of the problems with visual evidence is that very often our eyes see things differently at different times or are tricked altogether. The sky looks black at night but blue by day. A dress that appears white in sunlight may appear yellow by candlelight. Railway lines seem to converge in the distance. Things far away look much smaller. On hot days, illusory puddles shimmer on the road. The Greek philosopher Plato talked about how what we think of as reality may actually just be like shadows from a fire playing on the cave wall where we have been bound captive all our lives – when reality is the real objects revealed in bright sunlight. Plato proposed that beyond the shifting, imperfect world we perceive is another realm of perfect, unchanging Forms, an inner reality as brilliant as the sunlit world outside the cave that gives the shifting shadows their substance. Although philosophers have largely abandoned this Platonic vision, it has remained a source of fascination for fiction writers ever since.

The English philosopher John Locke got round the problem of illusions a different way. Human understanding, Locke suggested, is like 'a closet wholly shut from light, with only some little openings left, to let in external visible resemblances, or ideas of things without'. We don't actually see real things at all, even though they may be there, but instead create or 'represent' them in our minds from purely visual sensations. In other words, seeing a tree is like seeing a picture of a tree in our minds and seeing someone sit down beneath the tree is like seeing a film of it. If so, our painting of a tree may actually be said to be no less real than a 'real' tree, because it's simply a representation of the image of the tree the artist sees in his or her mind.

However, one of the problems of this 'representative realism' is that you then have to ask who's actually doing the watching. Descartes saw the mind effectively as a stage (later called the Cartesian theatre) on which ideas and perceptions are viewed by an inner observer or 'homunculus'. But just who or what is the homunculus, and who's watching inside the head of homunculus? It begins to sound like some absurd Russian doll.

That's why some philosophers, such as Berkeley, insisted that it was pointless to ask whether something had a reality outside our perception. There is no way we can be sure the world has any other reality. Berkeley insisted that '*esse est percipi*' – to exist is to be perceived. In other words, reality exists only as long as it is perceived. If I blink, reality disappears momentarily. But this, though quite logical, is solipsistic, and so counter-intuitive that we'd probably regard someone who genuinely believed it as slightly unhinged.

Maybe the best guess is that we do live in a world of real things, and that these real things are what cause our sense experiences, an idea known as causal realism. It sounds self-evident, but the crucial thing is that the real object causes the experience, so there is a direct link between the real thing and our sensory experience. It's an assumption which cannot be proved by logic – we cannot know we are not just brains in a vat – but it's the most fruitful way of treating reality, and there is no evidence to contradict it.

We are reasonably confident that when we look at a tree we are looking at a real thing, and this is borne out by others also seeing the tree – although they might see it differently. Similarly, we are reasonably confident in our sensory experience of a painting to say that we know the painting itself is real. Equally, we can be confident enough in our senses to say that the tree in the painting is not real, but simply a representation of a tree created by the artist. The tree may be a representation of a real tree, or it may be the representation of an imaginary tree, created in the artist's mind, maybe as a result of seeing real trees or being told about them. The artist chooses how to represent the tree – whether it's 'realistic' like a pre-Raphaelite painting, which the viewer instantly connects visually to a real tree, or entirely abstract like a tree by Picasso.

Does a snail have a consciousness?

(Experimental Psychology, Oxford)

This is such a seemingly simple question, yet it throws up challenges that have baffled both philosophers and scientists. One of the problems, of course, is defining just what consciousness is.

In commonsense terms, it just means being awake and aware. A snail, like most animals, is able to sleep and wake up. A snail is also, like other animals, aware enough of particular features in its environment to respond to them, choosing where it goes and how it reacts – even if it's only at its own particularly languid pace. But we know, from our own experience, that there is much more to consciousness than this.

The problem is how to get inside an animal's head and know just how it thinks. Consciousness is a very private experience. It's hard enough to know what consciousness is like for other humans, when we have the benefit of language and many other ways of communicating to tell us. It's almost impossible with animals, so we have to infer from things they do and the way they react.

There's always been a tendency for we humans to regard ourselves as rather special and different from other animals. While it's clear that physically we have much in common with other animals, we've also liked to think that our brains are somehow special, and many thinkers from Aristotle onwards have suggested that we are uniquely conscious. Sometimes human consciousness is described as 'self-awareness' – the idea that we know that we are conscious, and are aware of who we are. It used to be a commonplace that only humans recognised themselves in a mirror. But then it was shown that apes, elephants and dolphins do, and more recently even little magpies with their birdbrains have proved they can, too. Even though we might think it's unlikely, it's hard to imagine a test to prove for certain that a snail cannot recognise its own reflection. Moreover, there is no reason to assume that an animal, especially one so fundamentally different, experiences consciousness in the same way that we do – so even a proven failure of the mirror test would not prove anything about snails.

Over the centuries, countless philosophers from Descartes to Daniel Dennett have speculated on just what consciousness is, and for Descartes being aware of thinking was the single basic truth of existence. In recent years, the notion of consciousness has been explored by psychologists and neuroscientists, as well as thinkers about artificial intelligence. While philosophers try to work out just what it all means, scientists such as Francis Crick and Roger Penrose have tried to explain where and how it occurs physiologically in the brain.

Most thinkers agree that understanding consciousness is one of the hardest of all intellectual problems. In his 1989 *Dictionary of Psychology*, British psychologist Stuart Sutherland wrote: 'Consciousness is a fascinating but elusive phenomenon; it is impossible to specify what it is, what it does, or why it evolved. Nothing worth reading has ever been written about it.' Not everyone is quite as pessimistic as this, and there were small signs of progress at least in spring 2009, when French scientists showed that consciousness is a coordinated activity involving the entire brain – and not located in a particular place.

Recently, British psychologist Nick Humphrey suggested that animal consciousness may have started with the way a creature keeps track of its response to the environment and then evolved as the ability to privatise and internalise these tracking responses developed into a sense of self and a will to survive that gave the creature a competitive edge. If this is so, there is no reason to think that consciousness cannot have developed right through the animal kingdom, down to the level of snails. If snails have this kind of self-awareness, it's clearly nothing like as sophisticated as our own, but it might be a mistake to assume that they are simply rather gelatinous automata.

Thinkers on consciousness have sometimes divided it into two kinds, which were labelled 'access' consciousness and 'phenomenal' consciousness in 1995 by American linguist and philosopher Ned Block – although not everyone agrees there is such a division. 'Access consciousness' is being aware of information in the mind and being able to access it. 'Phenomenal consciousness' is simply experiencing things without any physical response. Feeling pain, tasting coffee, hearing music are all such experiences or 'qualia', as they are sometimes called. Some thinkers suggest that qualia are the difference between ordinary humans and zombies. Zombies have no qualia, so no inner life, and are thus nothing more than puppets.

In the 1970s, Thomas Nagel wrote a famous paper, 'What is it like to be a bat?' in which he summed up the experience of qualia as 'what it is like to be'. He then went on to suggest that we cannot yet imagine any way of knowing what it's like to be a bat (or a slug or any other animal, including humans) – and any physical theory of consciousness cannot be considered until we have some way of understanding this subjective experience of the world. This is sometimes described as the 'hard problem of consciousness' (as opposed to easier to understand access consciousness). Other thinkers, such as Daniel Dennett, deny the division of consciousness and the 'different' quality of qualia altogether, and believe that there is just one all-embracing kind of consciousness. At the moment, though, the answer must be that we know very little – less than the snail …

Why is there salt in the sea?

(Biochemistry, Oxford)

Well, strictly speaking, there isn't; there are only dissolved chemicals which combine to make salt when precipitated, and which give seawater a salty taste. So far, 72 separate elements have been found in seawater, and the chances are that nearly every natural element on earth is in there somewhere. However, the most abundant by far are ions of chlorine (about 55.3 per cent) and sodium (about 30.8 per cent), the elements that combine to make common salt. The other relatively common ions are magnesium (3.7 per cent), sulphur (2.6 per cent), calcium (1.2 per cent) and potassium (1.1 per cent). It's these six elements that make seawater salty or 'briny'.

On average, the salinity of sea water is about 35 o/oo, which means 35 parts salt to a thousand water. That's a huge amount of salt – the equivalent of a teaspoon of salt in a glass of water. Estimating the total volume of water in the oceans, you can work out from this concentration that overall there is a staggering 50 million billion tons of salt in the sea – and that if all the salt were extracted from the oceans it would cover the entire earth to a depth of 500 feet!

The salt concentration varies from place to place, though – as we know mostly from a worldwide series of chemical tests conducted in 1884 by William Dittmar aboard the British corvette HMS *Challenger*. It's highest in the Red Sea and Persian Gulf, and lowest in the Baltic and the Arctic Ocean. This variation gives us a clue about why there is salt in the sea in the first place. Levels are high in warm seas, where evaporation of pure water leaves salt behind in the water and increases salt content; and low in cooler seas, where pure water is continually added from melting ice and rivers.

The oceans probably formed originally as water vapour 'degassed' from the molten rocks that once covered much of the hot early earth, formed clouds and then rained as the earth cooled. The original ocean waters were pretty much freshwater, but the salt content gradually built up as salt was added from three main sources – rivers flowing into the sea, hydrothermal vents on the sea floor and undersea volcanoes.

Rain falling on the land (and the oceans) is pretty much pure water (made slightly acidic by dissolved atmospheric gases). That's why rivers are freshwater rather than salt water. Although they are usually fresh-tasting, however, rivers are never completely pure. Instead, they contain tiny traces of salts and other solids – some the fragments of weathered rock, others dissolved directly from susceptible rocks such as limestone as water seeps through the ground on its way to the river.

It's estimated that some 4 billion tons of salt are washed into the sea every year from rivers around the world. At that rate, it would take about 200–300 million years to give the oceans their salt content. The rivers don't dilute the ocean because just as they add freshwater, so freshwater continually evaporates from the ocean surface. That's why salinity tends to be lowest on the ocean margins where rivers continually flood in freshwater, and highest in mid-ocean. But why haven't the oceans got steadily saltier and saltier, then, as more salt is added and water evaporates? It's thought that they have now reached a balance where the salt content stays steady. Each year, much the same amount of salt is precipitated out of the oceans to settle on the ocean floor as is added to them by rivers.

Interestingly, 'freshwater' rivers tend to carry much more calcium, bicarbonate and silica than 'saltwater' in the sea. Seawater, however, contains much more sodium and chloride. One of the reasons for this is that marine life plays quite a significant role in the chemical balance of the oceans. A lot of calcium is taken out of seawater by the huge numbers of creatures such as molluscs, crustaceans, foraminifera and corals that use calcium to build skeletons and shells. Diatoms extract silica. Other creatures affect the chemical composition in subtler ways, such as snails that extract lead and sea cucumbers which secrete vanadium.

What is the point of using NHS money to keep old people alive? *(Economics, Cambridge)*

As the author Anthony Powell said, 'Growing old is like being increasingly penalized for a crime you haven't committed'. After decades of hard labour and long service to the government in the form of taxes, you finally start to get ready for a deserved rest – and what happens? Your body starts to play up and your senses start to weaken – and you can only sleep properly in the middle of a conversation. To add insult to injury, some people start to say that you are placing a burden on the health service. No wonder you might begin to mutter bitterly every now and then!

Of course, there is a serious point here. Old people are as deserving of health resources as anyone, if not more so, because they have paid their tax contributions all their lives. The ethos of the NHS is that it provides free health care for all, and old people should not be exceptions to this policy. It's quite simple; if they are ill, they should be treated.

Unfortunately, the NHS does not always live up to this ideal. A recent survey by the British Geriatric Society of British doctors suggested that more than half would be worried about how they might be treated when they were older – because of the way they see old people being treated now. Most doctors surveyed believe that older people are much less likely to have symptoms properly investigated. When old people feel ill, there is a tendency to assume that the problem is 'just old age' rather than examining them properly for signs of a treatable illness. Three-quarters of the doctors asserted that older people are less likely to be properly treated and referred to the right specialists.

Of course, many of the health problems faced by older people are an inevitable part of growing old. But this does not mean they cannot be treated in any way. Old people may also respond less well to treatment for some ailments than younger people do. It is therefore sometimes suggested that limited NHS resources should be steered towards younger people where they can give more obvious improvements to quality of life. Indeed, there is some evidence that this how the NHS does indeed respond, often treating old people as second-class patients. There are much longer waits, for instance, for hip and knee replacements, which affect primarily old people, than for other operations. Women over 70 are not automatically invited for breast screening as younger women are. And older women with breast cancer are less likely to receive the full range of cancer therapy than younger women.

In 2005, NICE, the body that produces guidelines on drug policy for the NHS, put the cat among the pigeons when it produced a report saying that, 'When age is an indicator of benefit or risk, age discrimination may be appropriate'. It fired an angry response from Help the Aged, who retorted: 'Assumptions that the life of an older person is somehow worth less, or that it is not important if someone who is nearing the end of average life expectancy receives less attention than people in their twenties or thirties, have been widespread. The [NICE] guidelines would run the risk of reinforcing such prejudice.'

It is perhaps understandable that this happens. On the face of it, it seems so much more worthwhile to pour the best (and most expensive) resources the medical profession can offer into treating a nineteen-year-old with all their life ahead of them, if the treatment is effective, than into treating an 89-year-old who is less likely to thrive, and likely to have only a short time of health before some other ailment strikes. Managers and doctors facing a heavy workload and limited resources may argue that choices have to be made and that such prioritising, though undesirable, is simply unavoidable. There is often an attitude, too, that old people have had their 'fair share'. More poignantly, sometimes doctors who treat old people with all the skill and dedication they would devote to younger patients are forced to accept that they are fighting a losing battle – that they will not be able to keep their patient alive, let alone restore them to good health. When, then, do they stop fighting?

But there is a problem with too much 'pragmatism'. The NHS is an ideal – the ideal of the best available treatment free to all, no matter who – and it's an ideal that should not be sacrificed lightly. For each and every patient and their loved ones, it's their health and their life that is precious. The ideal of the NHS means we should not be making choices between one person's health and another's. Every patient should be treated to the best of doctors' abilities. If this principle is compromised, it begins to undermine the important and reassuring comfort of knowing that we will always be treated when we are ill; it also begins to place a very difficult burden on doctors to choose who should be treated and who shouldn't.

Yet the NHS budget is rising by the year and the UK has a population that is ageing. Already over 20 million (more than a third of) British citizens are over 50 years old, and old people are more prone to illness. 55 per cent of 75–84-year-olds have some illness or disability and two-thirds of those over 85 do. It is argued therefore that this increasingly aged population will place more and more strain on the NHS's limited resources – and the ability of younger people to fund it – and that we need to start recognising this before catastrophe strikes. What this argument fails to recognise, however, is that the old people of today are much, much more healthy than those of former years. That is exactly why we have so many old people. And if there are numerically many more frail 90-year-olds now dependent on the NHS than in earlier times, there are also many, many more very fit people in their 60s still actively contributing to society economically, socially and intellectually. More importantly, a society that fails to look after its old people and hold them in any less than the utmost respect may be said to be sick and in need of treatment.

You have a 3-litre jug and a 5-litre jug. Make 4 litres. (Mathematics, Oxford)

This problem comes up in the movie *Die Hard with a Vengeance*. At the bidding of the monstrous Simon Gruber (aka Peter Krieg) (Jeremy Irons), John McCain (Bruce Willis) and Zeus (Samuel L. Jackson) are forced to solve this problem in order to disarm a bomb. They succeed just in time. They did it like this (using gallons rather than litres): First they fill the 5-gallon jug. Then they empty 3 gallons from the 5-gallon jug into the 3-gallon jug, leaving 2 gallons in the 5-gallon jug. Then they empty the 3-gallon jug and add the last 2 gallons from the 5-gallon jug. Then they fill the 5-gallon jug and fill up the 3-gallon jug, using just 1 gallon and leaving 4 gallons in the 5-gallon jug. *Et voilá!*

This problem is so simple that you can see the solution straight away, and the writers were clearly looking for a riddle that most of the audience would be able to work out or at least understand for themselves. But it's an age-old arithmetical problem based on the subtraction of relative prime numbers. Relative prime numbers are numbers where the only whole number that both can be divided by is 1. That doesn't mean that either is a true prime number, just that they can both be divided only by 1. Thus 15 and 16, although not primes, are both relative primes, whereas 15 and 21 are not, because they can both be divided by 3.

Euclid found a way to solve relative prime number problems like the *Die Hard* riddle 2,300 years ago. The proof is complex, but the arithmetic relatively simple, and it allows us to solve any similar problem, such as how you would get a 13-minute egg from a 5-minute and a 9-minute egg timer.

(You 'calibrate' the 5-minute timer to 4 minutes, by starting them both off together, stopping when the 5-minute timer runs out – leaving 4 minutes on the 9-minute timer – starting both off together again and stopping when the 9-minute timer runs out, leaving just a minute on the 5-minute timer. You can then cook your egg for exactly 13 minutes by starting with the 9-minute, then reversing the 5-minute timer for the remaining 4 minutes.)

All these solutions can be expressed by mathematical equations. If one of the measures you have is p and the other is q, you can find the solution you need, k, with the following equation. In this, m is the number of times you need to fill or empty p, and n is the number of times you need to fill or empty q.

$$mp + nq = k$$

If m or n is negative, it means emptying the jug (or egg timer); if m or n is positive it means filling the jug. In the case of the *Die Hard* jugs, p is 3 and q is 5. So you would get k is 4 if m is plus 3 and n minus 1.

$3 \times 3 + -1 \times 5 = 4$

That means filling the 3-gallon jug three times and emptying the 5-gallon jug once. Alternatively, you could go with m as minus 2 and n as plus 2, i.e. emptying the 3-gallon jug twice and filling the 5-gallon jug twice.

$-2 \times 3 + 2 \times 5 = 4$

Both of these are different solutions from John McCain's and require a third large jug as a reservoir, but they are equally valid solutions.

Was it fair that a woman's planning application for painting her door purple in a conservation area was declined?

(Land Economy, Cambridge)

The idea that our past needed protecting by law from the ravages of modernisation first emerged in the mid-nineteenth century. As mass industrialisation and urbanisation swept away age-old ways of life, many believed something valuable was being lost – not just old and often beautiful things but our whole connection to the past, intangible, fragile but immensely precious. It's no coincidence that the first great strides into the modern urban, industrial world coincided with the revival of the Gothic style of architecture, the medievalism of the pre-Raphaelite art movement and the emphasis on traditional skills of the Arts and Crafts movement.

The preservation movement began with the scheduling of Ancient Monuments in 1882 to protect important ancient archaeological and historical sites. In 1947, the realisation that unique old buildings needed protection too against demolition or simply being ruined by modernisation led to the idea of 'listing' buildings. Then conservation areas came in during the 1960s; battlefields, historic parks and gardens were placed on registers in the 1980s; and, most recently, marine archaeology has been given protection.

Conservation areas recognise that not just stately homes, ancient castles and quaint medieval cottages are part of our heritage but so too are whole neighbourhoods of 'ordinary' historic houses. The idea is to preserve the special historic character of these neighbourhoods. Yet conservation areas cannot be locked into the past like museums where the buildings are simply preserved 'in aspic'. They are usually places where people live, and people need the freedom to make their lives and homes as they want – not according to the diktat of a government heritage expert. Moreover, these areas have already long been lived in and altered piecemeal. So do you preserve them as they are now? Or do you restore them to what you think they were like when they were built or at a certain time in their history? And when things need replacing, as they often do, how far do you go in replacing them with their 'historic' equivalents? When the leaks in a 150-year-old slate roof finally become irreparable, for instance, do you replace it with expensive hand-crafted slate, or cheaper, more leak-proof modern equivalents?

There is no easy answer to these questions and they lead to constant disputes between owners of homes in conservation areas and the heritage authorities. For most conservation areas, local authorities publish clear guidelines about what they will allow in order to preserve the neighbourhood's special character. They may, for instance, forbid modern roof extensions, or the replacement of historic wooden sash windows with aluminium casements. It varies from area to area. Quite often, they will specify that the walls of a house in an area where all the houses are of natural stone or mellow brick may not be painted, or at least not in garish colours. This makes sense. Painting the house this way would not only destroy some of that particular house's special historic character but would affect the unified look of the entire street which is part of its appeal.

Does the same apply to something as 'small' as a purple door? Well, yes it could. If the special historic character of the street or neighbourhood depends on subtle, pastel colours or even natural wood in the doors and window frames, a bright purple door could well stand out like a gap tooth and mar the overall effect. And the 'overall effect' is important. The idea is to preserve these areas for the benefit of all, not just those living there. Of course, painting a door is not necessarily a permanent change that destroys any of the historic fabric, and the owner might argue that it's her choice entirely what colour she paints the door of her own house. But the whole concept of conservation areas means that property owners within those areas give up some of their own individual rights to change their property in order to preserve the areas' historic nature for the good of the community at large.*

It could be argued that everyone has an absolute right to do with their own property as they will. However, most would agree that a society in which there are absolutely no mutually agreed rules on planning could not only be ugly and chaotic and unpleasant to live in – but would be in constant battle as neighbours got into dispute when someone built a strip club next to a children's nursery, or a steel furnace towering over someone's quiet cottage garden. Building controls are agreed by consent, and in theory, at least, democratic local and national elections give people the chance to challenge controls they don't agree with.

---

* The woman might argue that in the historic past she might have been able to paint the door as purple as she pleased, so the pastel look is not necessarily any more 'historic'. But the aim in conservation is not usually to recreate an imagined historic past but to preserve the patina of time passing – that's the crucial difference between the real thing and a faux-historic recreation. Of course, this is a source of constant debate among building conservators. When things need replacing, how far do you go in replacing them with some presumed or even thoroughly researched historic equivalent?

The same is true of conservation rules. It's the individual's choice to live in the conservation area. If the woman really has to have a purple door, yet it's not allowed in a conservation area, then she must probably live elsewhere.

That said, it may be that some of the rules in a conservation area are unreasonable – and restrict individual freedom just too much. After all, a historic area might lose its life and much of its character if it was robbed of all individuality and change. So a careful balance has to be struck, and perhaps with the woman and her purple door the conservers might have been a little too restrictive, presenting a blank bureaucratic face rather than responding with careful consideration.

There is, of course, no definitive line about what should be preserved and what updated, so the system must not just allow continual debate but actively encourage it. Maybe if purple-door woman felt that she was listened to and that her paint choice was denied to her not by faceless bureaucrats but people who actually cared about the place she lived in, just maybe she might actually *want* to paint her door in a more subtle colour rather than feeling aggrieved because she was forced to. Or maybe the authorities would change their minds ...

Do you think Chairman Mao would have been proud of the China of today?

(Oriental Studies, Cambridge)

When Chairman Mao died in 1976, he left behind a country in turmoil. Instead of the shining future he had promised, he had led China into the most catastrophic, tragic decades in its history. The scale of the disaster Mao had brought and the sheer misery is unimaginable. His master-plan for the economy, the Great Leap Forward (1958–61), in which he collectivised all farms and set up steelworks across the country, brought an agricultural downturn and famine so appalling that it claimed the lives of at the very least 40 million people. As if that weren't enough, retiring to the back seat in admission of his failure, he then launched the Cultural Revolution in which Mao's Red Guard of young people ravaged China's heritage and killed, imprisoned or drove into exile hundreds of thousands of China's brightest minds in their attack on the 'corrupting' and 'bourgeois' citadels of culture.

The China of today would have been almost unrecognisable to Mao. Bourgeois culture has arrived with a vengeance. So too, for some, has the prosperity Mao promised but never delivered. Beijing is one of the most dynamic, fastest growing cities in the world. So too is Shanghai. All across the country, there is a whirlwind of construction as the old towns are cleared away for the multi-lane expressways, glitzy shopping malls and shimmering sky-scrapers that are a symbol of the new China.

In one way, China seems to be hurtling down the route to being a consumer society like a runaway juggernaut, in a seeming triumph for Western values. On the other, it remains in the iron grip of the Communist Party. More people live without an elected government in China than do in all the rest of the world put together. At the same time as China seemed to reach the pinnacle of its new prosperity and confidence with the Beijing Olympics in 2008, so it showed its darker face in July 2009, with the disappearance of ethnic Uighur protestors that sparked a tragic series of reprisals against the Han Chinese identified with the government.

Of course, it's impossible to say whether Mao would have been proud of China today. He was so enigmatic in his lifetime that even his best friends could not guess what he was thinking. It would be absolute folly to think that one could guess now he has been dead for more than three decades.

Mao was a firm believer in communism and an implac-able enemy of the bourgeoisie and imperial culture. His thoughts expressed in the *Little Red Book*, his determined collectivisation against all odds and his resolute attack on culture all suggest a mind so set on his own unique version of Marxism-Leninism that it seems he could not possibly approve of the opening of the country to the capitalist enterprise which has changed China's fortune. Moreover, that opening was driven by Deng Xiaoping, the man who though once his comrade in arms had become his chief political opponent and one of the prime political targets of the Cultural Revolution. And Deng had only managed to achieve his 'Open Door' policy with Mao safely dead and his erstwhile allies the Gang of Four consigned to prison. Everything points to Mao being such an unyielding enemy of capitalism and the bourgeois culture that seems to be engulfing cities like Shanghai that he would have been appalled. There are certainly hard-line party members today who oppose the changes in China by invoking the ghost of the Chairman.

And yet maybe that's all too simple. Just as Deng came to believe that bringing prosperity to people was more important than maintaining strict ideology, it's just possible that Mao might have done in time, too. After all, his professed desire in joining the Chinese revolution was first and foremost to improve people's lives. It might be said that many of his moves, against Deng as against intellectuals, were as much political as ideological. Maybe if he could claim responsibility for China's recent achievements, then he would be proud.

To talk about China's achievements is not to deny the problems. Rural poverty is still widespread. Peasants frequently suffer such economic hardship that family lives are ripped asunder as fathers and mothers, sons and daughters, sisters and brothers are forced to live apart much of the year as they travel to the cities to seek work. Political freedoms are still curtailed. Cities are rife with exploitation. And yet, China is already the world's second largest economy after the USA, and is its fastest-growing. Hundreds of millions of Chinese already live in the kind of comfort and affluence that would have astonished people just a few decades ago. Since the country's economic reforms began in 1978, 400 million people have been lifted out of poverty, and the number of people living in absolute poverty (less than a dollar a day) has been cut by more than 90 per cent. Moreover, while China's average income still makes it a poor country, it has achieved a level of literacy and life expectancy equivalent to middle-income countries like those of Eastern Europe. Former head of the World Bank Paul Wolfowitz observed when he visited China in 2005 that 'East Asia has experienced the greatest increase in wealth for the largest number of people in the shortest time in the history of mankind'.

It's almost certain that Mao would have no problems with the level of political control and lack of democracy that people in the West criticise China for. After all, it was he who put many of the controls in place. It's almost certain he would turn a blind eye to the environmental damage now so widespread in China. But maybe he would have been immensely proud of China's extraordinary economic achievements – no matter how they arrived and despite the problems among the peasants who were always the focus of his attentions. Maybe, standing atop one of the world's tallest buildings in Shanghai, travelling the world's fastest train from Shanghai airport, or watching China's own space probes soar into the stratosphere, he would puff out his chest and boast in an uncharacteristically loud voice about just how far his very own revolution had brought China.

Why isn't there a global government?

(Philosophy, Politics and Economics, Oxford)

Countless times through the ages thinkers have wondered if all the world's problems might be solved if there was just one government for the entire world. The logic is simple. Wars seem to be fought at the behest of governments and rulers. So if there was just a single government or ruler, there would be no wars.

> *For I dipt into the future, far as human eye could see,*
> *Saw the Vision of the world, and all the wonders that*
>   *would be;*
> *... Till the war-drum throbb'd no longer, and the battle-*
>   *flags were furl'd*
> *In the Parliament of man, the Federation of the world.*
> *There the common sense of most shall hold a fretful realm*
>   *in awe,*
> *And the kindly earth shall slumber, lapt in universal law.*
> Alfred, Lord Tennyson, 'Locksley Hall' (1837)

It's such a beguiling vision that it crops up again and again in both fiction and philosophical and political thinking through the centuries. Back in the thirteenth century in *The Banquet* (*Convivio*), Dante argued that war would end if 'the whole earth and all that humans can possess be a monarchy, that is, one government under one ruler. Because he possesses everything, the ruler would not desire to possess anything further, and thus, he would hold kings contentedly within the borders of their kingdoms, and keep peace among them.' In his *Leviathan*, Thomas Hobbes talked of cooperation between governments around the world, an idea developed by Charles-Irénée Castel, Abbé de Saint-Pierre into a European federation in which sovereigns gave up their power to achieve 'perpetual peace'. Rousseau, though, believed that such a union would never occur without violent revolution, and any institution that came into being that way would do more harm than good – a speculation that was borne out, in some ways, by Napoleon's attempt to unite Europe under the French Revolution, which ultimately served only to unite nations in opposition.

Immanuel Kant talked a great deal about world government, and believed the culmination of human history to be 'an international state (*civitas gentium*), which would necessarily continue to grow until it embraced all the peoples of the earth'. However, he also argued that, as things stand, 'the positive idea of a world republic cannot be realised', because of the messy mix of monarchies and despots in the present world in which individual freedoms are far from guaranteed.

The appalling conflict of the two world wars of the twentieth century revived an interest in global government – or at least world forums. After the First World War, the victors convened the League of Nations, while after the Second World War they created the United Nations. Both of these might have governed the world by consent between individual nations, but in reality had almost no control because some nation states, such as the USA and the USSR, have proved far too powerful and self-assertive to pay much heed to the UN – an example followed even by smaller nations such as North Korea, Iran and Burma which have effectively ignored UN rulings.

In the aftermath of the Second World War and, in particular, the atomic bombing of Hiroshima and Nagasaki, there was perhaps the most serious political attempt in history to form a real world government. Albert Einstein was just one of many high-minded campaigners who were so disturbed by the problems of nuclear weapons that they believed a world government was the only way forward. 'A world government must be created which is able to solve conflicts between nations by judicial decision,' Einstein wrote. 'This government must be based on a clear-cut constitution which is approved by the governments and nations and which gives it the sole disposition of offensive weapons.'

Ironically, one reason why Einstein's vision never had a chance of reaching fruition was because of the stand-off between two ōpposing power nexuses and ideologies, both of which in their own way sought to bring the world under a single banner. On the one side was the Soviet Union, fuelled by Lenin's vision of exporting communism to the entire world and dreaming of creating a world socialist economy governed by a 'Bolshevik World State'. On the other was the Western world led by the USA, which sought a transcendence of nation states and capitalism around the world. The communist vision seems to have all but vanished now in face of the seeming triumph of the West, and Francis Fukuyama talked confidently in 1992 of 'the end of history' as the entire world moved towards liberal free-market democracy – the prelude in Kant's view to world government. Yet, of course, the recent financial crisis and continued political turbulence around the world has shown that such optimism was ill-founded.

In some ways, the world *has* moved towards more coordinated government, if not world government. All of Europe is now under the federation of the European Union, for instance, and countries all round the world join in economic and political pacts with their neighbours. More and more, nations are attempting, superficially at least, to cooperate on key issues such as trade and the environment. While the UN may seem to be only a little more than a talking shop, Gordon Brown's 2009 coordination of measures to deal with the banking crisis and global recession was a tangible example of joint action by consent that is persuading experts to talk not of global government, but global governance – in which the world is not controlled by a single world government, but by coordinated transnational action under the direction of organisations such as the World Trade Organization, the G20, the IMF and so on.

Underlying it all, of course, is the behind-the-scenes power of globalisation. Economic and communications links around the world are now so strong that nations are no longer able to act entirely by themselves, while the financial clout of global corporations and banks is such that the affairs of the world are, in many ways, directed and governed on a global scale independently of national governments. In some ways, it might be said that we already have global government *de facto* in the hands of global economic powerbrokers, even if not *de jure* in the hands of an official world government. It's in the interests of such people to keep global governance away from governments (especially global governments) – and they argue that, on the whole, the effect of too much government power is to restrict free trade and enterprise and so stifle economic growth. When France's Nicolas Sarkozy and Germany's Angela Merkel recently argued for tough global policing of banking practice, the USA and UK won the argument against them, insisting that such policies would almost certainly deepen the recession – and no doubt the financial powerbrokers breathed a sigh of relief.

Back in the 1940s and 50s, when Einstein was campaigning for world government, George Orwell and Aldous Huxley created their dystopian visions of how global government might actually turn out in *Nineteen Eighty-four* and *Brave New World*, visions of soulless worlds in which there was no room for the individual. In the face of the monolith of the Soviet Union, that fear seemed all too real. Kant argued that the main problems with world government in the present world were that it might either be too powerful or too weak, and the fear that it might be too strong seemed uppermost.

Like Orwell and Huxley, many people, at least in the West, have feared the power of over-arching government. The continued distrust of many ordinary people in Europe of increasing federalisation of the European Union shows how deep-rooted this fear is. The UK's Labour government are generally committed to greater European integration, yet they have had to tread very carefully with the British public, avoiding, for instance, a referendum on the Lisbon treaty – fully aware that they would face an uphill battle to get it accepted. If people cannot be persuaded to accept integrated government in Europe where liberal democracy is universal, the chances of achieving it on a global scale seem remote indeed.

To most people around the world, the firmest attachment beyond family and neighbourhood is to their historic nationality. While they are willing to give their consent to be governed by their own national government, made up of people of their own nationality, speaking their own language, they tend to resent what they see as interlopers from transnational governments. Hence, Lithuania, Estonia, Latvia, Georgia and many other parts of the Soviet Union were quick to stake out their right to independence as soon as the USSR broke up, while Scotland has asserted its own right to govern itself within the UK.

With this kind of nationalism, a voluntary political union of the world seems as remote now as it did in Dante's time. The British Empire brought the world closer to world government than at any time during history, controlling a quarter of the world, but it was never a voluntary union and broke up as soon as the centre proved weak enough to lose its grip, leaving new nations such as Australia, Canada, New Zealand and India to emerge.

And yet an interesting thing happened recently. The election of Barack Obama as President of the USA was greeted with almost universal acclaim around the world, and Obama has become something of a hero. On a visit to Ghana in early July 2009, Obama was welcomed by crowds so enthusiastic that it was as if he was their leader, not the leader of the USA. Ghana is the rising star of African democracy – which is maybe why Obama avoided its more democratically challenged neighbour Nigeria – and one gets the feeling that if Obama was to stand as president of Africa, he would be elected by a landslide in free and fair elections. And if he was to stand as president of the world, maybe he would be elected, too. Of course, this is unlikely to happen, but such speculation suggests that world government may not be such an impossibility after all.

Back in the mid-nineteenth century, US General Ulysses S. Grant, reflecting on the triumph of the American federation after the Civil War, commented: 'I believe at some future day, the nations of the earth will agree on some sort of congress which will take cognizance of international questions of difficulty and whose decisions will be as binding as the decisions of the Supreme Court are upon us.' Only time will tell.

Is the Bible a fictional work? Could it be called chick lit? (English, Oxford)

What a strange question this is! The first part about the fictional nature of the Bible seems intriguingly provocative. The second part about whether it's 'chick lit' seems simply bizarre. It's hard to imagine anything less like chick lit than the Bible.

The term chick lit apparently came into being in the later 1980s on American college campuses as a way to describe the female literary tradition – presumably authors such as Jane Austen, the Brontës and so on. But in the 1990s it acquired its present tag as new women's fiction, targeted at 'chicks' (young white women) about 'chicks' (hip, contemporary, fashion-conscious, career-driven, sex-obsessed young women). No one in the Bible remotely fits that bill – except perhaps Samson's paramour Delilah, and John the Baptist's nemesis Salome. Women generally have a very subordinate role in the Bible, and are immoral when sexual, like Lot's daughters, and wicked when ambitious. Even though sympathetic, strong women do appear in the Bible, they are stoic rather than determined, maternal rather than seductive. The Bible is a 2,000-and-more-year-old collection of books written mainly by men living in a very traditional society. There is nothing at all chick lit about it even by the furthest stretch of the imagination. Mind you, it does have enough incest, violence, bestiality, murder, betrayal and special effects to satisfy the most demanding horror movie fan …

Whether it's fictional or not is a much more interesting question. Most church authorities long ago conceded that not every single word is literal truth. Only a minority of more fundamental Christians, for instance, believe that God literally created the world in seven days with all the creatures of today fully formed. The Bible stories are, for many believers, metaphors rather than actual fact. But that doesn't necessarily make it all a fiction. Movies like *Braveheart* and *Schindler's List* are entirely imaginary, yet are based on real historical characters, while movies like *Titanic* and *Pearl Harbor* place fictional characters within real historical situations. Even stories like *Harry Potter* blur fiction and fact, using real locations such as King's Cross station then adding imaginary details like platform 9¾. In fact any history, where it tells a story, however closely based on real events, tends to blur history and fiction – with the historian filling in the blanks here and omitting other details there. Moreover, there is often an irresistible temptation to colour the events of the past to make a good story, or reassess their impact with the benefit of hindsight. Many historians have tried to avoid this 'Whig' history, but it's almost impossible to be entirely objective unless you simply present historical documents. So even if the Bible has fictional or metaphorical elements, that would not necessarily make it a fictional work.

The New Testament is essentially about Jesus and his life, and the events that followed. It's mainly written in the form of Gospels and Epistles. *Gospel* is a word meaning 'good news' while *Epistle* means 'letter' and this gives a clue to the intention, at least, of the writers. They do not present themselves as authors intending to create a fictional story, but as reporters and correspondents spreading a news story or giving an opinion piece. Their stories are not told in the breathless matter-of-fact style of modern journalism, nor are they, we might guess, cross-checked for factual accuracy – though we have no way of knowing this; the Gospel writers may have been rigorous in checking their sources for all we know.

Yet the Gospels, at least, are often meant to be based on reports of eyewitness accounts or, at least, rumour and hearsay. Even if it's merely hearsay and turns out to be utterly meaningless (or even invented by some mischief-maker), it does not turn the Bible into a work of fiction

– simply a very flawed piece of reporting. The Bible writers wanted us to believe that these events really happened. Jesus is presented as the true Son of God, who really did live on earth, not as a fictional character. The things characters in the Bible say are almost certainly not verbatim records, but they are probably intended as plausible versions of what they might have said. So even if the dialogue is largely fictional, it does not make the Bible a fictional work – more a docu-drama that is taking (maybe undue) liberties with the smaller truth, with, the authors might claim, the intention of revealing a larger truth.

Historians have found almost no other historical sources to cross-check the Bible and verify its story. Yet little has been found either that denies its story. Recent archaeological finds have shed light on its history and suggest that some of the people and locations featured are real, and some of the events described really happened. But that may make it no truer than *Braveheart*, or even stories about King Arthur or Robin Hood. That's why some Bible scholars argue that the Bible is not meant to be an accurate historical document, but rather a work of literature and theology inspired by historical events and stories. It's a question of faith how much you believe is literal truth.

Is feminism dead? (Classics, Cambridge)

As long as there are women alive, so will feminism be, since there will always be a woman's perspective on every issue. But the term 'feminism' has particular connotations. It originated in France in the 1880s and was introduced to Britain in the 1890s to stigmatise those campaigning for women's rights, but it was widely adopted by the women's movement only in the 1960s and 70s when 'Women's Liberation' or 'Women's Lib' acquired too many negative overtones, associated with strident public demonstrations and notoriously 'bra-burning'. So when *Time* magazine famously asked 'Is feminism dead?' in 1998, they were not necessarily asking if the women's movement was dead but if it was true of the 1960s and 70s brand – the feminism of women like Germaine Greer, Gloria Steinem and Sheila Rowbotham, the feminism that introduced the notion of sexism and the sex war. This phase of feminism was campaigning not just for women's rights to be recognised but for men's entire attitude to women to change.

It's usually the funeral rites for this particular brand of feminism that *Time* and many subsequent questioners have asked are due. Just as the Suffragette movement lost its momentum in the 1920s once votes for women were achieved, so the high-profile feminist campaigns of the 1960s and 70s seemed to have run out of steam by the 1990s as they achieved many of their goals. In the UK, the Equal Pay Act of 1970 was introduced to mandate equal pay for equal work, regardless of gender. Then the Sex Discrimination Act of 1975 protected women from being discriminated against in employment, vocational training, education, the provision and sale of goods, facilities and services, premises and the exercise of public functions.

By the 1990s, it seemed, women were beginning to take it for granted that they would be accepted in the workplace and might reach the top of their chosen profession (although the picture has not actually proved quite so rosy). Sexism was widely regarded as a term of abuse. Abortion on demand was enshrined in law in many countries. And maternity leave was becoming more and more generous. What's more, younger women were throwing off the apparently drab, dungaree-wearing, bra-burning intellectual feminism of the 1970s to have fun with 'Girl Power', epitomised in the media by the Spice Girls – sassy, fun, in-yer-face and openly sexual in a way that would have appalled the older generation of feminists who hated the portrayal of women as sex objects.

The writer of the 1998 piece in *Time*, Ginia Bellafante, pointed the finger of blame, too, at Camille Paglia's 1990 book *Sexual Personae*, in which she argued that female sexuality was humanity's greatest force and that it was up to women to realise its power. Bellafante lamented that in the wake of Paglia's highly publicised proclamation of female sexuality, feminism was melting away in a welter of self-indulgent sexual and romantic confessions, in which a woman only had to proclaim she enjoyed sex – or complain that her love-life was bad – to be lauded by other women for expressing a woman's perspective. Bellafante lamented too the popularity among women of *Ally McBeal* and

Bridget Jones's Diary, both of which portrayed the apparently self-indulgent emotional life of 30-something single women – examples, Bellafante felt, of the dead-end into which feminism had strayed.

A report by sociologists at Cambridge University published in 2008 seemed to confirm that things have moved on even further since the 1990s and that many women are beginning to reject feminism. It isn't just that many women dislike the label 'feminist', which seems to have the same dry, hidebound, rather insulting overtones as the expression 'politically correct' – another product of 70s politics. It's as if many women are actually doubting some of feminism's core values. The Cambridge report suggested that support for gender equality had peaked in the 1990s but is now in decline. Back in the 1990s, over 50 per cent of women thought it was right for women to work rather than look after children; now it's barely 40 per cent (under 40 per cent in the USA). According to the study's leader Jacqueline Scott, professor of empirical sociology, 'When it comes to the clash between work and family life, doubts about whether a woman should be doing both are starting to creep in'.

Then a few months later, a report in the *British Medical Journal* led by Professor Jay Belsky suggested that more than twice as many children who were in day-care for more than twenty hours a week were insecure compared to those cared for full-time by their mothers. A recent government report found that toddlers spending more than 35 hours a week in day-care were prone to be more aggressive than their non-nursery peers. It seems more and more women admit to enjoying pornography and are happy to embrace pole-dancing as a form of exercise and self-confidence boost – something that would have horrified an earlier generation of feminists. The emphasis has shifted away from a general political movement, it seems, to self-help. The only battles a woman has to fight, it seems, are not with society but with her own self-esteem.

There are certainly some women (as well as smug men, of course) saying that we are now in a 'post-feminist' era. Some women say the idea of feminism is irrelevant in a society where gender equality has, apparently, been achieved. Others such as Naomi Wolf say that they are post-feminists because they are taking charge of their own future rather than putting it in the hands of a political or academic movement. Indeed, they want to shake off the stigma of being labelled a feminist. The 'glass ceiling', the invisible barrier that seems to prevent women being promoted above a certain level, is just that, they say – glass, which can be easily smashed by a determined woman.

Yet there are many women who believe that feminism is far from dead. Even if well-to-do white women in the West are having doubts about where it should go, women around the world still face far too many problems. Back in the 1990s, some women argued that feminism should move on from the second wave of feminism – the feminism of the 1960s and 70s which campaigned for equal opportunity at work (the first being the suffragettes who campaigned for the vote) – and begin what Rebecca Walker (bisexual African-American daughter of *The Color Purple* author Alice Walker) called the third wave.

The third wave, they argued, should not seek to drive every woman towards the white middle-class ideal of the supermum, but should allow all kinds of different directions, which included non-heterosexuals and women of colour. Authors Jennifer Baumgardner and Amy Richards wrote in *Manifesta* that: 'We're not doing feminism the same way that the seventies feminists did it; being liberated doesn't mean copying what came before but finding one's own way – a way that is genuine to one's own generation.' Some of these third-wave feminists are willing to embrace female identity in whatever shape or form it takes, including sex-work. What matters to them is challenging oppression. Critics of the third wave, especially those among the older generation of second-wavers, suggest that it lacks focus and cohesion. But third-wavers argue that they are simply adapting feminism for their generation, the generation of hip-hop, pop culture, consumerism and the internet, not Kennedy, Vietnam and Woodstock.

Many of the battles feminism fought in earlier decades have indeed been won, and the feminists of the 1960s and 70s have every reason to be proud of their achievements. Yet all around the world, there is still much to do before women really are treated equally to men. Women still rarely achieve the highest roles in politics, for instance. The UK's

Margaret Thatcher and Germany's Angela Merkel are still the only women to have become leaders of major Western powers. Women are still in a small minority as elected representatives at both local and national levels. And a scan of the faces at the UN shows just a handful of women among a sea of men. Moreover, average pay levels for women remain significantly below those for men. In many countries, the difficulties women and girls face are much worse, ranging from enforced circumcision and enforced marriage to sexual exploitation and barred access to education and careers. Until all these problems are solved, feminism even as a solely political movement can never be dead.

What percentage of the world's water is contained in a cow? *(Veterinary Medicine, Cambridge)*

Of course, there's no way you can answer this question easily unless you have a few basic facts, and even then you'd only be able to make rough estimates, not accurate calculations. And yet with those few basic facts, you can make a pretty good stab at the answer to what at first seems an impossible question. For a little more on the value of estimates to apparently impossible questions, see 'What's the population of Croydon?'

Whatever the answer to this bovine hydration question is, you know it's going to be very small. The number of cows on the planet has increased dramatically in the last few decades as more and more people around the world turn to meat and dairy products. There are now about 1.3 billion cows on earth – that's one cow to every four or five people. So the percentage of water in a single cow of all the water in just cows alone is much less than a billionth of a percent, or 0.000000001 per cent.

Most people know that the human body is largely water – about 70 per cent by weight – and the chances are that other mammals have pretty much the same water content. You could guess that the average cow weighs about 500 kg, which would mean it contains about 350 kg of water – that is, about 350 litres. So that's easy enough.

It's much harder to come up with an estimation of the volume of water in the world. The best way is probably to ignore all the freshwater, ice and atmospheric moisture (which is less than 3 per cent of the total) and concentrate on the volume of water in the oceans. Assuming that about three-quarters of the earth is covered in water, you can work out the area of the oceans from the formula for the surface area of a sphere, which is 4 times pi times the radius squared, or $4\pi \times r^2$. The radius is about 6,400 km. Squared that's about 41 million. Four times pi is about 12.5. So the surface area of the earth is very roughly 500 million square kilometres. Three-quarters of that is about 360 million square kilometres. The oceans are probably about 4,000 metres deep on average. So the volume of the water in the world is 360 times 4,000 cubic kilometres – that is, 1,440,000 cubic kilometres, or 1,440 million billion litres.

So to work out the percentage of water in the cow, we divide the volume of the world's water by the volume of water in the cow and multiply by 100. The answer is about 0.00025 billionths of a percent, or 0.0000000000025 per cent.

Although this is an entirely academic exercise, the connection of cows and water is an important one. Raising cows for beef is incredibly demanding in terms of water. Not only do cows drink a lot of water, they consume food which takes a lot of water to grow, and slaughtering them and processing the meat takes a lot of water, too. It takes on average nearly 5,000 litres of water to produce just one quarter-pound beef burger – 1,000 times as much as for the same weight of wheat. So if you were to eat just two burgers a week for a year, it would take half a million litres of water. If just one in ten of the world's population ate the same number of burgers as you, then you'd need 300,000 billion litres of water to produce the beef for them. That's a huge proportion of the world's freshwater – not far short of a fifth! This is why some people worry that we are in for a major water crisis if beef consumption goes on rising as it is now.

If you're not in California, how do you know it exists? (Geography, Oxford)

On a practical, everyday basis, it makes no sense to challenge the existence of California, even if you're not there to experience it directly. You can cross-check its existence from many different sources – some eminently trustworthy, such as important reference books and atlases, some perhaps less trustworthy, such as, say, your next door neighbour. There are not just written accounts, but photographs as well of places within California and photographs of the entire state from space, not to mention all those Hollywood movies, California raisins and bottles of rosé wine.

What's crucial is that every source you try will usually confirm that California exists. It's highly unlikely that any source at all will say California does *not* exist. What's more, you could ring up someone in California and ask them to confirm that it's still there. In fact, from your knowledge of the rest of the world, you could probably be pretty confident that there was at least something in that space between the Pacific and the American midwest.

Of course, it might all be an incredibly elaborate subterfuge – a worldwide conspiracy designed to fool you into believing in California, for instance, or an elaborate holographic mirage that even 'visitors' and 'residents' in California are completely convinced by. Or you might just be delusional. But with such multiple, varied sources of information, the odds are so completely stacked in the favour of California's existence that for all practical purposes you can assume it exists – until you have evidence to the contrary.

Philosophers have always had a problem with how we know things, and it seems there is nothing, logically, that we can really be certain of.* Even Descartes' famous bottom line, 'I think therefore I am', has been shown subsequently to be flawed. So of course you cannot ever be completely certain of California's existence, even if you are there to experience it directly. However, most people would accept Plato's less absolute idea of knowledge, explained in his dialogue *Theaetetus*, as 'justified true belief'.

Plato argued that there are three elements involved in knowing something. First that the fact is actually true; second that you believe it to be true; and third that you are justified in believing it to be true. So if California does exist (and its existence is not questioned here), then you can say that you know it exists if you believe it does exist and are justified in that belief. The justification comes from the overwhelming weight of evidence demonstrating its existence, and the discovery that every method you could conceive of disproving its existence will fail.

---

* It's tempting to see a parallel between the California question and Berkeley's famous philosophical riddle, 'If a tree falls in a forest and no one is around to hear it, does it make a sound?' (Or, in other versions, 'does it really fall?') But Berkeley was arguing that things exist only if they are perceived, and, of course, there are plenty of witnesses to California's existence. Berkeley, as an empiricist, would accept the validity of the empirical evidence. What he would argue, however, is that, logically, California would cease to exist if all witnesses to its existence vanished: 'To be is to be perceived.'

Justification usually comes from three sources: empirical (the evidence of the senses), authoritative testimony and logical deduction. In asserting that you know California exists, you are relying almost exclusively on authoritative testimony, since you cannot be there and see for yourself and you can logically deduce its existence only in a very loose way.

The great Austrian-British science theorist Karl Popper (1902–94), however, argued that justification isn't enough, and that scientific theories and other claims to knowledge should always be rationally criticised. What is important, Popper argued, is that a claim must be falsifiable – that is, a claim can be accepted as knowledge only if it's possible to show that it's false. Thus a belief in God can never be knowledge because God's existence cannot be disproved. Good scientific theories can be, and scientists must always strive to disprove them – and you should work from the assumption that they are probably false. In other words, if you follow Plato's reasoning, the best claims to knowledge are those that are likely to be true; if you follow Popper, the best claims are those that are least likely to be untrue. So, by Plato's book, you can say you know California exists from the weight of authoritative testimony that shows that it does. By Popper's, you can merely say that you can find no evidence that it does not.

While it's always wise to question one's assumptions, and Popper's arguments for continual rational criticism are powerful, it's simply impractical to question everything, and the reality of California is something it's not worth questioning. Say you wanted to take a trip to Hollywood. You might not know for certain that California exists, but if you refuse to get on the plane until you do know, you'll spend your entire life in the airport lounge. No one will catch you out being wrong, but, my goodness, you'd soon get bored with tasteless snacks and the mind-numbing muzak!

When are people dead? *(Medicine, Oxford)*

Traditionally, people were declared dead when their hearts stopped beating, their blood stopped circulating and they stopped breathing. So doctors would listen for a heartbeat, or occasionally conduct the famous mirror test to see if there were any signs of moisture from the potential deceased's breath. In popular parlance, when people's hearts stop and they breathe their last, they are dead. But in the last half-century, doctors have proved time and time again that they can revive many patients whose hearts have stopped beating by various techniques such as cardiopulmonary resuscitation (CPR) and fibrillation. So a patient whose heart has stopped can no longer be regarded as dead. Instead, they are said to be 'clinically dead'. Someone who is only clinically dead can often be brought back to life.

The limit to resuscitation is that when the heart stops, the lack of blood circulation immediately begins to damage the body – especially the brain. Normally the brain can only survive without severe damage for less than three minutes after circulation ceases – although if the patient is very cold it can survive much longer, especially if the patient was very, very cold before their heart stopped. The longest documented survival was of an infant child who stayed submerged beneath the icy waters of a frozen lake for 40 minutes, and recovered completely. Some clinicians think that extreme cold may enable children to survive without brain damage up to an hour after clinical death.

Once the brain is badly damaged, however, there is no hope of revival, so many legal definitions of death focus on brain death – although some religious groups prefer the traditional version. By brain death, doctors usually mean the cessation of all brain activity due to the destruction of neurons from the loss of blood circulation. The problem is to determine when this happens. Doctors now accept that death is a process in which various bodily functions gradually shut down rather than a single event, so there is no one moment of death.

However, it's often crucial to ascertain the exact moment of death. For instance, if the deceased is an organ donor, the donor organs must be removed from the body as early as possible after death, since most are quickly damaged once circulation stops. So doctors conduct a physical examination to check for absence of signs of brain function. Tests differ, but they focus essentially on absence of response to pain and absence of any reflexes in the cranial nerves, the nerves that lead direct to the brain from senses in the head such as the eyes. They test, for instance, if the pupils respond to changes in light intensity or if the patient blinks when the eyelids are touched.

Tests like these are good enough for a doctor to be confident that the patient is dead, but a second doctor must confirm the results, and sometimes there must also be no signs of electrical activity in the brain recorded by two EEGs (electroencephalographs) for 24 hours before the patient can be declared legally dead.

Complications arise, however, because many conditions can mimic brain death, such as drug and drink intoxication and coma from traumas. So there is considerable confusion and controversy over a patient who shows no clear sign of brain activity yet retains blood circulation – even if that is artificially maintained. Particularly distressing and confusing are persistent vegetative states in which, to all intents and purposes, brain activity seems to have ceased, yet the blood is circulating, the patient is breathing and the eyes are open but just not taking anything in. Many news stories have focused on grieving families who ask for life support to be withdrawn from coma victims in a persistent vegetative state who show no signs of ever regaining consciousness, yet cannot be declared legally dead. Gunshot victim Gary Dockery suddenly awoke in 1996 and started speaking normally after eight years in a vegetative state, but his recovery proved short-lived. He lapsed into silence after just 24 hours and died less than a year later.

Circumstances like this aside, there are some situations in which it's absolutely clear that a person is dead, particularly when violence is involved. The media also talk about how victims of accidents and violence die 'instantly'. That is rarely quite true if the body remains intact, though. Some believe that even decapitation victims may remain conscious for some seconds after their head is removed, for instance. Only if the body is completely destroyed in an instant will death also be completely instantaneous. Otherwise, it's a gradual process – either very rapid, or much slower. However, once your corpse has been cremated or your buried cadaver has been victimised by worms, you can be pretty certain that at least your physical body is dead …*

Chekhov's great, isn't he?

(Modern and Medieval Languages, Cambridge)

Yes, perhaps the greatest writer of the last hundred or so years. Only Ibsen and Shakespeare have a status equal

---

* When Michael Jackson died on 25 June 2009, it was just a matter of days before someone claimed on the internet that it was all a cover-up. The real truth is that he simply faked his death and has gone into hiding to escape the pressures of celebrity – just like, of course, Elvis Presley, Tupac Shakur, Jimi Hendrix, Jim Morrison and Amelia Earhart, not to mention King Arthur, Jesus Christ and many others whose death somehow lacked finality. So some people are never quite dead, while others such as Count Dracula and the average zombie are just non-committally undead.

to Chekhov as a dramatist, and some of his short stories, particularly *The Lady with the Dog*, are among the greatest little masterpieces of the genre. What was extraordinary about Chekhov was the remarkable skill with which he conjured the inner life of people in both his stories and his plays.

Before Chekhov, most stories moved forward through events. Things happen to characters, and they react to them, and the stories tend to end with a neat flourish – lovers united, friends divided and so on. But in Chekhov nothing much ever happens. Things might, but somehow they never quite do. In *Uncle Vanya*, Yelena and Astrov might have an affair, but they don't. Vanya might shoot Serebryakov, but he doesn't. In *The Lady with the Dog*, we feel almost certain that Gurov and Anna Sergeyevna, even after waiting so long, will not finally live happily together ever after. The plays and stories all tend to peter out as if we've somehow missed something. There is never any satisfying climax. And yet this does not seem undramatic. What is unsaid, what is undone, is so much more powerful and emotive than any more sweeping, eventful story.

Chekhov's great skill is in portraying the character's inner tug of emotions through what they don't say and what they don't do. When Sonya and Vanya resume their routine work at the end of *Uncle Vanya*, for instance, they say little and just get on with life again as if nothing has happened and nothing will ever happen. Yet the tragedy of their loss – and the certainty that they will never escape their small lives – is palpable. The stories resonate deep within us in a way that superficially bigger stories rarely do because they feel so close to our sense of life – how we all have much larger inner lives and hopes than we can ever express or enact.

Chekhov is astute enough to realise that this failure to bring our deepest dreams to reality appears absurd and almost comic, which is why he described his plays as comedies even though they seem to be about lives steeped in failure and futility. Few writers are able to create with such subtlety the humour of someone's absurdity at the same time as the poignancy of the flaws that make them so comic.

The extraordinary thing is that by diminishing the events that happen to the major characters, Chekhov enlarges the role of the minor characters. In *The Three Sisters*, for instance, the loneliness of the comic Kulygin is as affecting as that of Olya, Masha and Irina. Minor characters are not there to help the plot along, but to create a complete emotional inner world in which everyone is both linked by similar aspirations and divided by a huge gulf in communication.

Telling a story on stage not through events but through the inner lives of characters was such a dramatic innovation that at first people just didn't get it. Earlier in the nineteenth century, Henrik Ibsen had shaken the theatre world by moving drama away from big historic and romantic stories about heroic figures to naturalistic dramas about ordinary domestic situations and disputes. Yet Ibsen's plays are still driven along by what people say or do. Chekhov shifted the ground so dramatically towards characters' inner lives that it demanded a whole new way of acting.

When *The Seagull* was first staged at the Alexandrinsky Theatre in St Petersburg on 17 October 1896, the result was disastrous. Acted in the conventional way, it just seemed like a really bad play with absurd characters and no real plot. The audience booed and Chekhov resolved never to write for theatre again. Fortunately, the theatre director Vladimir Nemirovich-Danchenko recognised Chekhov's potential and persuaded his colleague Constantin Stanislavsky to direct it for the Moscow Arts Theatre.

In directing the play, Stanislavsky developed an entirely new method of acting in which actors tried to bring the 'subtext', the unspoken inner life of the characters, into being, by focusing not so much on what the characters say, but what they want to say – their 'intention'. Stanislavsky was trying to create a stage process in which characters were both intensely naturalistic and psychologically real – a process which demanded huge attention to even minor details. Chekhov hinted that the checked pattern of the trousers of Trigorin, the writer in *The Seagull*, mentioned only in passing, is one of the keys to an actor finding the truth of the character.

Restaged by Stanislavsky in 1898, *The Seagull* suddenly took flight and Chekhov went on to write three other great plays – *Uncle Vanya*, *The Cherry Orchard* and *The Three Sisters* – which have ensured him his place in theatre history. Stanislavsky's System of Acting proved hugely influential during the twentieth century and was the inspiration for the American Method acting style which allowed actors to bring such psychological realism to film roles especially. The intense, naturalistic style of acting we have come to take so much for granted in film, where everything is viewed in close-up, owes everything to Chekhov's plays, via Stanislavsky and the Method. Without it, actors would still be declaiming like Olivier and Gielgud.

There is something deceptively simple about Chekhov. When characters speak they speak in such mundane language, in such banalities, and the events in the plays are often so trivial, that it seems as if the plays must be easy to write. Vladimir Nabokov wrote of Chekhov's 'medley of dreadful prosaisms, ready-made epithets, repetitions'. But that is exactly how things need to be, because that is what traps the characters, and the great poetry in Chekhov's work lies in the unsaid, the linking web of emotions that underpins the surface banalities. It might seem easy, and yet no one since has achieved the same thing. Chekhov's four great plays and his handful of short stories stand as an unequalled pinnacle of psychologically real, profound storytelling.

What is the population of Croydon?

(Geography, Cambridge)

At first sight, this seems a rather pointless, uninteresting question that only a resident of Croydon or someone with a complete and detailed memory of the National Census could possibly answer.

But stop to think a second. You can actually make a guess. You might guess that the population of London is some 10 million. You might guess that there are some 30-odd boroughs in London. So, instantly, you might guess that the population of Croydon is 10 million divided by 30 – that is, about 333,333. In fact, if you did make a guess this way, you would be astonishingly close; the population of Croydon in 2007 was 336,600! So with a simple guess that took no more than a few seconds, you have got within about 1 per cent of the true figure. There was an element of luck in getting quite this close, since London's population is actually less than 10 million and it happens to have 32 boroughs, not 30. But the point is that you can make a pretty good stab quickly and without access to any figures whatsoever.

In fact, making a rough, commonsense estimate from a few basic facts is a surprisingly useful skill not just in everyday life but even in high-level science, and that's what makes this apparently routine question so fascinating. What you might call a 'guesstimate' or a 'back-of-an-envelope' calculation, physicists call a 'Fermi problem', after the great nuclear physicist Enrico Fermi, who took a legendary delight in posing and solving such problems, such as 'How many piano tuners are there in Chicago?'

During one of the first atom bomb tests at Trinity in New Mexico in 1945, Fermi famously estimated the power of the bomb by dropping a few scraps of paper as the shockwave passed and seeing how far they travelled as they fell. The scraps fell some 2.5 metres away, so Fermi guessed the blast was about 10 megatons. In fact, Fermi's estimate was too small, since the blast turned out to be over 18 megatons. However, he had got within the right order of magnitude with just an incredibly simple, instant calculation. This is what makes guesstimates so valuable.

Making a guesstimate of the answer you expect before you embark on a long, complex scientific calculation, for instance, can reduce the chances of making a massive error simply through a wrongly inputted figure or miscalculation. Alternatively, a guesstimate can help you get a useful 'ballpark' figure even where numbers are huge and real figures are effectively unobtainable. That's the basis of the famous Drake equation, devised in 1960 by Dr Frank Drake to estimate the likely number of intelligent civilisations in our galaxy. The fact that we haven't actually encountered any of these civilisations is known as the Fermi paradox – to which the somewhat nihilistic answer is often that these civilisations lasted just a short while before self-destructing …

Beyond the academic world, guesstimates can provide valuable hints of possible policy flaws even without long and extensive research. In their book on guesstimation, Lawrence Weinstein and John Adam show, for instance, how you can make an instant estimate of how much crop-land would be needed to replace petrol with corn-based ethanol as motor fuel – an estimate which suggests instantly how ultimately unworkable the idea might be. Many management consultants and financial businesses also now use estimation questions, such as 'What is the market for toilet rolls in China?', to test the intelligence of job candidates and their ability to think on their feet.

Interestingly, Croydon's population has been in the news recently because Croydon council challenged the calculation of its population by the Office of National Statistics. According to ONS figures, Croydon's population has increased by barely 0.5 per cent since 2001, whereas Croydon council found that the local need for housing and schooling suggested a larger increase. Apparently, the ONS count was affected by changing the way it counted international migrants. The discrepancy was not just a matter of statistics, since Croydon's general government grant, like that of all local councils in the UK, is given per head of its population. So an underestimate of population would mean a smaller grant.

Finally, the question, 'What is the population of Croydon?' does not necessarily require an answer in numbers. If you interpret it as meaning, 'What is the *nature* of Croydon's population?' for instance, you open up a whole new range of possible answers. It might be that you talk about the population's racial background, which in some areas of the borough is increasingly mixed. Or you could be talking about the age structure. A philosopher might even answer the question 'What is the population of Croydon?' existentially …

Why are big, fierce animals so rare?

(Biological Sciences, Oxford)

This deceptively simple question gets right to the nub of the intricate, interdependent interrelationship between all the world's living organisms. Big, fierce animals are large predators like lions, tigers and polar bears that are big and fierce because they need the strength and ferocity to kill and eat other fairly big creatures to survive. Polar bears prey on smaller animals such as seals. Lions prey on grazing animals such as zebras and antelopes.

Big animals like these need to eat a lot of meat, and must have plentiful prey. So large predators must inevitably be fewer in number than the creatures that they prey on. Indeed, nature ensures a fairly constant ratio between predators and prey. If the prey numbers ever expand, there is more food to sustain predators and so predator numbers expand – ultimately limiting the number of prey. If prey numbers shrink, predator numbers shrink too because there is less available food, until the ratio settles down again.

Of course, the large predators' prey need to eat, too, and large predators are often at the top of a long chain of animals that feed upon other living things – or rather a pyramid, because the numbers get bigger and bigger the further down you go. So for every polar bear, for instance, there needs to be at least, say, ten seals. And for every seal there needs to be about 40 of the herring that they eat. Then for every herring, there needs to be 800 or so of the zooplankton called copepods that they feed on, while for every copepod there needs to be about 24,000 of their phytoplankton dinners. That means that to feed just a single polar bear you need a vast pyramid of organisms supported by nearly 8 billion phytoplankton! It's hardly surprising, then, that big, fierce creatures are few in number.

In fact, they are even fewer in number than this simple numerical relationship might imply. Biologists refer to the different steps of the food pyramid as 'trophic levels' (from the Greek *trophe*, meaning food). Feeding and eating are essentially energy exchanges, and the fundamental laws of thermodynamics mean that each time energy is exchanged some is lost in the form of heat. So as you move up from one trophic level to the next, there is always a loss of energy.

The initial energy input usually comes from sunlight, which is used by 'autotrophs' (self-feeders) – essentially plants – to convert chemicals in the environment into food. All other living things are heterotrophs, which means that they depend on this initial energy input, either by eating the plants directly, or by eating other living things that eat the plants and so on.* No wonder, then, that big, fierce creatures are few in number.

Being at the top of the food pyramid also makes large predators particularly vulnerable to environmental shocks. Whenever there is any disruption of the habitat, the problems reverberate up through the pyramid and the top predators are usually first to suffer. As human activity has had more and more impact on the natural environment in the last century, for instance, large predators have become not just few in numbers but genuinely rare, as their habitats, and so their food supplies, dwindle. The human inclination to hunt and kill big, fierce creatures has reduced numbers still further. Sabre-tooth tigers are believed to have been driven to extinction 10,000 years ago by human hunters in North America. Today, the combination of environmental threats and hunting means that there are very few big, fierce creatures that are not just rare but actually in severe danger of extinction.

Are there too many people in the world?

(Human Sciences, Oxford)

This is a loaded question which divides opinion sharply. The world's population is certainly bigger than it has ever been before. There are now (in July 2009) some

---

* This includes decomposers and detritivores such as bacteria and fungi which live off dead or waste matter.

6.77 billion people in the world – and three or four new ones are joining us every second. With such a gigantic, and rapidly growing, population, it's easy to see why some prophets of doom predict that it will all end calamitously when the number of people simply becomes too great for the finite resources of the earth.

The idea of 'overpopulation' dates back to Thomas Malthus in the early nineteenth century. Malthus argued that it was easy for human population growth to outstrip the earth's capacity to sustain it, and people began to talk of a 'Malthusian catastrophe' – the dramatic crash in population that would inevitably follow once the limits to growth had been reached. At the time Malthus was writing, the world's population was under a billion, but the onset of the Industrial Revolution set in train a remarkable swelling of human numbers to more than 3 billion by the 1960s – with no sign of any global Malthusian catastrophe.

That, though, was when some economists began to ring the alarm bells. Paul Ehrlich wrote a bestseller called *The Population Bomb*, which predicted imminent doom, while in the early 1970s a group going by the name of the 'Club of Rome' produced a report called *The Limits to Growth* full of tables with equally dire forecasts. Yet the outcome in the decades since has confounded their pessimism. There are now more than twice as many people crowded onto the planet as there were when Ehrlich was writing – far, far more than his predicted catastrophic limits.

One reason why the calamity has not yet arrived is a revolution in agriculture which has dramatically boosted the world's food output. So although over a billion people suffer from lack of food, the problem is how the food is shared, not the total quantity. And yet the arguments of the over-population doom-mongers seem in some ways to be just too much like plain common sense to ignore. Surely there must come a time when there are just too many people in the world for its resources?

Scientists and economists have now begun to argue about just what the earth's 'carrying capacity' for humans is – and most suggest a maximum of between 10 and 20 billion. Current population forecasts by the US census predict that we'll begin to reach those ultimate limits in just 40 years' time. So if there are not too many people in the world now, there will be soon. Some scientists, however, argue that the notion of human carrying capacity is false and that human innovation will find ways to sustain an ever greater number of people. The repeated failure of dire predictions in the past seems to give that argument some sustenance.

And yet, the world is already – right now – facing manifold serious, and potentially disastrous, problems which can be directly attributed to pressure on the earth's resources. The spectre of global warming, for instance, is now quite clearly attributable to the growing impact of human activity on the planet, while the pressure on water and food resources is at crisis point in many places around the world. Moreover, the natural world is going through a sharp phase of mass extinctions as animals are muscled out of their environmental niches by humans. It's unarguable that these problems are real, and serious, and happening now. Does this mean, then, that there are actually too many people in the world already? Well, not necessarily.

The problems are as much to do with the way the world's resources are used as they are with a simple equation between population numbers and resource capacity. Global warming, for instance, has been driven by the massive growth in energy use which has gone hand-in-hand with the rise in human population over the last half-century in particular. Yet it's the way energy is used that is a problem, not the sheer number of people. In fact, quite a small proportion of people in the developed world are responsible for the massive energy consumption that has started the global warming ball rolling. Most of the world's population has played very little part as yet. So even a dramatic fall in the world's population would not necessarily ease the problem of global warming – unless the remaining few changed their consumption patterns. And a rise in the world population does not necessarily have to bring further global warming.

Of course, it's easy to imagine that a quiet, unpressured world in which there was plenty of space and resources for all would be a kind of nirvana. People often look back wistfully on the days when England had a population of just a few million and dream of how blissful that might be if we had all the comforts of modern living to go with that rural expanse. There would be no need for green belts to stop city development, and each of us could have large houses with larger gardens to expand in. And yet most of the great things we associate with human progress – science, technology, democracy, the arts, living standards and so much more – have grown with the world's population. They are the fruits of civilisation – of the growth of cities, of a dynamic urban milieu, of the bustling, booming, growing mess of humanity crowding together in ever greater numbers.

It is, perhaps, attractive to imagine more space for oneself, a bigger, more gently divided share of the world's scarce resources. But just who is 'too many', then? Who is to say? How many of us would ever say, I am one of the thousand, the million, the billion, too many? Most of us, rightly, consider ourselves infinitely precious – and none of us, however disadvantaged, however ill-starred, is 'too many'. What matters, of course, is how we treat each other and the world.

How many animals did Moses take on the Ark? *(Natural Sciences, Cambridge)*

Of course, this is a trick question or perhaps a slip of the tongue.* It wasn't the Biblical Moses who built the great

---

* The question does not necessarily assume, of course, a familiarity with the Bible, let alone a belief in it – just sufficient cultural knowledge to be aware of the Biblical stories.

Ark but Noah! The only ark that Moses was linked to was the Ark of the Covenant, the sacred chest said to hold the Ten Commandments. So if you answer how many animals did Moses take on this Ark, the answer would be 'very few – and most would be tiny stowaways such as insects'. That's not a very interesting answer, so after mentioning this it makes sense to move swiftly on to Noah …

The answer to the 'Noah' question all depends, of course, on how literally you take the story. And the question, of course, takes us right to the heart of the debate between Creationists, who argue that all animal species were created ready-made by God, and scientists who accept that species have evolved gradually from the simplest life forms over billions of years. Let's go along with the story to start with.

Noah, as every child brought up with the Bible knows, took two of every kind of animal on the Ark, the ship he was instructed to build by God to save them from the Great Flood that was coming. Everyone remembers the song:

The animals went in two by two, Hurrah! Hurrah!
The animals went in two by two, Hurrah! Hurrah!
The animals went in two by two, the elephant and the
  kangaroo,
And they all went into the ark, for to get out of the rain.

Not everyone remembers the last verse, however, in which the animals go in seven by seven, or if they do, they think it's just part of the song. In fact, it reflects what Genesis says Noah's actual instructions were – to take two of every 'unclean' animal, but seven of every 'clean' animal. Some Biblical scholars say that the seven means seven animals, others that it means seven pairs.

The real arguments, though, start over the number of kinds. Creationists who take the Noah story literally will tell you that Noah took one pair of every kind of animal. They get round the sceptic's argument that it would be impossible to fit even one of all the world's millions of species on any boat by saying that 'kind' means 'family', not species – and that evolution began after the Flood, so every kind of dog today, for instance, from coyotes to spaniels, is descended from the original Ark pair of hounds. That way, they say there would need to have been only a few thousand animals on the Ark to account for all the species alive today. Some of these believers suggest that the kinds even included dinosaurs, and kinds of every other now extinct animal.

Of course, all these arguments are utterly meaningless to evolutionary scientists. To most of them, the story of the Ark and the idea that all species were created ready-made is simply a myth, so any answer is fanciful. For rational scientists, though, the question about the Ark could spark an interesting hypothetical debate about how many animals you would need to fit on an imaginary Noah's Ark if you were to get two of every species alive today.

The remarkable fact is that even with all the research facilities and technology at our disposal, all the countless hours of diligent research and exploration, we have no idea how many species are alive on earth today, let alone throughout evolutionary history. Scientists' estimates suggest that there are at least 3 million species. There could be 30 million and there may even be up to 100 million. We can be confident we know most of the larger species of vertebrates, of which there are only about 50,000 species. But it's likely we know fewer than 10 per cent of all the millions of smaller invertebrates which comprise 97 per cent of all known species. There remain many millions of creatures as yet unidentified – too small to spot easily, living in remote, inaccessible places, or simply too elusive to have yet been noticed. All these, only nature would remember to bring on to the Ark.

How many grains of sand are there in the world? (Physics, Oxford)

This is a venerable question that dates back to the time of Ancient Greece. There was an old Greek proverb which talked about the amount of sand in the world as being so large that the grains are beyond number. It was, if you like, the ancient world's description of infinity. But as early as the third century BC, the great Greek scholar Archimedes sought to challenge the idea that the number of sand grains was infinite and inherently unknowable. In his famous book called *The Sand Reckoner*, Archimedes showed that though the number of grains of sand in the universe is, of course, uncountable, it's not incalculable.

Our modern (Indo-Arabic) numbering system provides a neat way of handling and writing very, very large numbers simply by adding a place for every step in magnitude of ten. We can even put them in shorthand by expressing them in powers of ten. But this was far beyond the numbering system of Ancient Greece, in which every number was simply a separate letter of the alphabet, giving just 27 possible numbers. Undaunted, Archimedes devised his own numbering system in *The Sand Reckoner* by taking the largest Greek number, the myriad (10,000) and creating multiples of myriads until he got to a myriad myriads (100 million), and then a myriad myriads times a myriad myriads (10,000 trillion). He then went on to estimate the number of grains of sand it would take to fill a universe which he assumed to be spherical, and with a radius of the distance then known between the earth and the sun. The answer he came up with was 10^{63}.

More recently, geologists Horn and Adam made a serious attempt to work out the number of grains of sand in the world, by making an estimate of the total volume of sand in all the world's sedimentary rocks, in all the world's deserts and on all the world's beaches. They calculated that there are 147 million cubic kilometres of sand, and by making assumptions about average grain size and packing, they hit on a figure of 875 trillion trillion for the number of sand grains in the world. A little while ago mathematicians at Hawaii University estimated the length, width and depth of all the world's beaches added together, and announced that there are 700,500 million billion grains of sand on all the world's beaches!

Although it's impossible to know the number of sand grains in the world accurately, modern research techniques, from satellite surveys to seismic studies, allow us to refine such calculations to a degree where we at least have confidence that they are in the right order of magnitude. But as our estimates become more accurate so there is less and less point in making them. As Archimedes strove to demonstrate, if the number of grains is knowable it can't be used as anything but a purely poetic image of the infinite. Moreover, as our knowledge of the universe expands both on the very largest scales and the very smallest scales, we have been introduced to all kinds of other unimaginably large numbers, from the number of stars in the universe (10 trillion trillion) to the number of atoms in your body (7,000 trillion trillion). The concept of infinity, however, remains as elusive as ever, and continues to intrigue mathematicians as they struggle to resolve the paradoxes of the finite and the not finite.

Was Romeo impulsive?

(Modern and Medieval Languages, Cambridge)

Of course Romeo was impulsive. We see it in the speed with which he switches to Juliet from his old love Rosaline, so:

> *That fair for which love groaned for and would die,*
> *With tender Juliet matched is now not fair.*

We see it as he risks sparking a deadly feud between the Capulets and Montagues for the instant gratification of his love for Juliet. We see it in the way he kills Tybalt in revenge, regardless of the consequences, actually calling for help to abandon sense, shouting:

> *Away to heaven respective lenity,*
> *And fire-eyed fury be my conduct now!*

And we see it in the extremity and suddenness of his love for Juliet, which even she is startled by, saying:

> *It is too rash, too unadvised, too sudden;*
> *Too like the lightning, which doth cease to be*
> *Ere one can say 'It lightens'.*

And, of course, this is exactly as Shakespeare intended; both Romeo and Juliet are the epitome of rash, impulsive youth, the personification of thoughtless, unconsidered love – which is both immensely appealing and ultimately disastrous.

But is it love that makes Romeo impulsive or is it because he is impulsive that he falls in love so readily? Love is so often described as a kind of madness, and falling in love can drive apparently sane men and women to the most extreme acts of folly. To many of the characters in the plays of Shakespeare and his near contemporaries, such as Lope de Vega and Calderón de la Barca, love and madness are flipsides of the same coin, a sweet madness. Even Freud admitted, 'One is very crazy when in love'. For romantics, the madness of love was liberating because it freed one from the bonds of normal behaviour.

Yet it's quite clear that Romeo is born to be a lover. He is looking for love, for the rush of adrenaline it brings. He is in some ways addicted to love, and addicted to being impulsive for the same reason. It is of course in the character of so many tragic heroes from Oedipus to Othello to act rashly, not stopping to think, driven by their hearts and not their heads. If only they stopped to think, maybe, things wouldn't have turned out so tragically.

But that is half their appeal to an audience, for they thus appear brave and passionate, even rather foolhardy, and watching them is excitingly dangerous. As we watch in fascination, there is always a tug between saying, 'No, don't do it! That's madness!' and 'Yes, throw caution to the winds and go for it!' that keeps us on the edges of our seats, deeply involved in all their ups and downs. Their impulsive-ness draws us in, in a way that more controlled, measured behaviour never would. They are risk-takers, intoxicating for an audience who take risks by proxy. But of course the risks they take make them prone to fall. That is what gives the audience an exhilarating emotional journey, but their failure reassures us that our more balanced approach to life is ultimately right, saving us from their tragic fate.

The Greek philosophers had a word for this kind of behaviour, *akrasia*, which gives us the word 'crazy', and understanding it has preoccupied both philosophers and psychologists ever since. For the Greeks, it was behaviour which goes against sense – not madness, but a lack of self-control, of knowingly doing something you think is not good for you. Why on earth would you do that? Socrates believed that the only explanation was ignorance – if people really know what's good for them they will behave accordingly. That's a view echoed today by many modern economists such as the late Milton Friedman. But that's not true of Romeo, who knowingly shuns the safe course. Thomas Aquinas took a more moral attitude, asserting that impulsive, excessive behaviour was a lack of the restrain-ing modesty of virtue, a lack of shame, or as the Greeks described it, *aidos* – something Nietzsche later castigated as a fatal weakness and absence of vision.

During the eighteenth century, philosophers began to look on impulsive behaviour in a more positive light, seeing it as coming from our untamed, natural side, and counterbalancing our more schooled, rational selves – the noble savage with simple instincts compared to the calculating elaborations of the civilised man. Freud took it much further, suggesting that impulsive behaviour came from the 'id', including basic subconscious drives such as sex that often conflict with the rational, conscious self of the 'superego', with the 'ego' in the middle trying to balance their demands.

Although Freud's ideas are no longer in vogue, many psychologists still think of a dual process in which human behaviour is torn between two different ways of thinking – a logical, language-based mode and a more irrational mode governed by associations. In this way of thinking, Romeo's behaviour is tipped towards the impulsive by all the powerful associations that have formed in his young mind between excitement and danger, pleasure and love. Even his language is engaged not by logic, but by the associations of love with everything of beauty, so that Shakespeare puts on his tongue some of the most wonderful, heady words of romance ever said.

> *But soft! What light through yonder window breaks?*
> *It is the East and Juliet is the sun!*
> *Arise fair sun and kill the envious moon.*

No wonder Juliet swoons.

How would you describe a human to a person from Mars? (Medicine, Cambridge)

Since the general consensus is that no one has encountered a person from Mars outside the realms of fiction – though of course followers of UFOs would demur – it's probably reasonable to assume that the question is intended as a hypothetical one. Of course, if I were talking to a 'real' Martian, I'd be trying to find points of reference in my description that the Martian would understand. If the Martian were rather human-like, this would be pretty simple. If the Martian were basically a living rock and had never encountered any other life-form than rocks, this might be a little harder. And, of course, without a common language, my task would be even harder! In fact, until the nature of this hypothetical Martian is known, the range of possibilities and difficulties is infinite and the question pointless.

I could go off on a flight of fancy, imagining my own kind of Martian and my own way of describing humans to this ill-informed alien, but my suspicion is that the questioner is trying to elucidate a description of humans rather than imagine our Martian friend. In other words, the Martian is irrelevant to the answer, and the idea is to describe humans to a completely unknown entity that we have no real contact with except via some interplanetary internet that translates perfectly but is, for some reason, unable to send pictures or anything other than a verbal description – a kind of weird obverse of the famous Turing test, in which a human questioner puts questions to a computer and tries to decide if the answers are coming from a computer or a living human.

Even so, it's hard to know where to begin without establishing some points of reference with the Martian. I could perhaps start with the simplest physical facts by describing the chemical basis of life on earth. Life on earth, I could say, depends on the remarkable ability of some large molecules of carbon to self-replicate and organise themselves into colonies. Life forms on earth are basically communities of self-replicating carbon molecules, each typically housed in its own sustaining package or cell. Over billions of years, these communities have diversified tremendously, as groups of cells develop their own specialised role. Now the variety of forms these communities take is enormous, although there are two major forms – plants, which are unable to move by themselves, but can obtain their sustenance from sunlight, and animals which can move but must actively seek food. Most animals have a head at one end containing a brain that controls their movement, a body containing the organs that they need to sustain themselves, and, usually, appendages to enable them to move.

Humans are complex animals that developed quite recently in earth's history – no more than 150,000 years ago. They have a head, a body and four limbs like many other animals, but unlike most others, they stand upright on just two of them, which means they can use the other two for grasping on to things, and their eyes, their visual apparatus, can look directly at what they are grasping. This gives them an enormous physical advantage over other animals in controlling their environment. But they have become unique in other ways. They dominate planet earth and manipulate their environment in a way that no other animal does.

They have developed complex brains, the ability to communicate sophisticated messages through language, and a level of self-awareness far beyond other animals, and this has enabled them in many ways to transcend the purely physical. They need to satisfy basic material needs such as food and warmth to keep themselves alive. But for most humans, life is so much more than just staying alive.

We humans can think about abstract ideas. We have imagination. By working together, and working separately, we can create a fantastic array of things to make life easier, from houses to live in to machines to move us around or to make tasks easier. We can create wonderfully elaborate things such as the varied sounds of music that have no other purpose but to entertain, stimulate or fill us with pleasure at their beauty. We have boundless curiosity which has allowed us to understand something of the nature of the world around us, building amazing machines to see far beyond our physical limits into the minute world of subatomic particles and the immensity of the universe, and formulating equally amazing theories to explain them. We have the ability to be both unutterably cruel to each other, and inspiringly caring. We have much in common, but each of us is slightly different, not only physically but also in our thoughts and needs, our hopes and fears. We are at the same time very simple creatures who have basic needs for material comfort, and complex beings who constantly worry about our place in the world. We sleep, we eat, we love, we talk, we work, we think, we analyse, we rant, we dance, we mope, we laugh, we cry.

Our lives are short and ultimately quite similar, but each lives it differently, each has his or her own inner life, dreams and fears, hopes and disappointments. In fact, we treasure our frailties, saying they are 'only human' because, when they don't cause us heartache, they impel us to learn, to explore, to adapt and to find ways of communicating ... even with imaginary Martians.

What do you like most about the brain?

(Medicine, Cambridge)

What a question! What I like is that someone can pose this question and that I can try, however ineffectively, to answer it. I like not what the brain is but what it can *do*. I like the fact that it enables me to think, to analyse and respond to experience, to formulate ideas and to know what pleasure is, and pain. I like the fact that it gives me my life.

I can't say I especially like it physically. In fact it's a little bit disgusting to look at. But I like the fact that with it

I can contemplate that this big dollop of paté contains a microscopic network of nerve cells that make it the most fantastically complex thing in the universe. Estimates vary wildly, since of course no one has counted them all, but there are some 100 billion separate cells in the human brain – which is, by strange coincidence, much the same number as there are galaxies in the universe. But this bald number, however awesome, doesn't begin to capture the almost miraculous complexity of the brain, with each of those 100 billion cells making 1,000 or more separate connections with other cells – and unimaginably more alternative pathways for nerve signals to crackle, fizz and buzz along as they make us jump up or sit down, laugh and cry, love and hate, sing, shout, swear, eat, drink and do everything that makes us human.

I like the way it's continually defying expectations and proving a more wonderful mechanism than a few scientists would have us believe. There was a time not long ago, when scientists portrayed it as a dying machine, a computer that gradually lost its effectiveness as you went through life, as old nerve cells died off and were never replaced. Using techniques such as fMRI (functional Magnetic Resonance Imaging) scans, scientists have now discovered that the brain is not simply a failing machine that steadily loses its working parts. Instead, it's a flexible, living organism with an amazing capacity for change and development through-out your life. It's said to be 'plastic' – that is, it can go on programming and reprogramming itself almost limitlessly.

I like the fact that it has become clear that your mental powers have very little to do with the number of brain cells that you have. It's the connections between them that matter – and there is an almost infinite possible number of connections between brain cells, at any age. Indeed, your brain goes on making more and more of these connections as you get older, not fewer. I like too that while you may lose brain cells as you get older, some, at least, can actually grow again. And losing brain cells may actually be good for mental powers, not bad. When you're a child, your brain evolves as it learns through repeated mass extinctions of little-used brain cells that allow those that prove their use to develop properly – a Darwinian 'survival of the fittest' process called apoptosis. Losing brain cells as you get older could actually be the brain's way of improving efficiency – cutting away the dead wood to allow the good to flourish.

But perhaps the brain's best victory over the reductive scientists is the recent discovery that its performance is in your control to a much, much greater extent than we ever realised. It has become clear that the future of your brain is at least partly in your own hands, or rather, your own thoughts. What I like best of all about the brain, though, is the fact that I have one, just like everyone else's but unique to me.

Why do so few Americans believe in evolution? *(Human Sciences, Oxford)*

It's one of the strange anomalies of the modern world that the USA, one of the most technologically advanced of all nations, should have so many uncompromising Christians who challenge some of science's best-established theories.

On a simple level, those who believe in the literal truth of the Bible, which describes how God made all the world's creatures at a stroke, must inevitably disagree with the theory of evolution, which suggests that all the world's living things evolved naturally over billions of years. But there is more to this question than that. Although there have been tussles, there are many Christians all around the world who are quite happy to accept the theory of evolution, without feeling their basic beliefs compromised.

The USA, however, is different. Recent surveys suggest that more than half of all Americans entirely reject the notion of evolution. In fact, in a survey of the US plus 32 European countries, Turkey and Japan, it turned out that fewer people in America accepted evolution than in any other country but Turkey. And when it comes to acceptance of Darwin's theory of natural selection, in which evolution progresses in an entirely automatic, mechanical (entirely God-free) way, the numbers shrink further – with only 14 per cent of Americans agreeing with it. Yet this idea has been accepted by scientists for not far short of a century.

It may be that many Americans are simply not suf-ficiently educated. The more people seem to know about science, the less unnerving they find the notion of evolu-tion. Yet a study by Miller, Scott and Okamoto published in 2006 in *Science*, backed up by a recent Gallup poll, suggests that it really is religious beliefs that are at the heart of the issue. Regardless of education, over half of American non-churchgoers believe in evolution, while less than a quarter of churchgoers do. However, non-belief in evolution does seem to go hand-in-hand with strongly conservative poli-tics and a pro-life stance – and moral certainty rather than spirituality. So it seems likely that the American distrust of evolution is maybe as much cultural as purely religious. There is a broad section in American society (proved to be in a minority, at least for a while, by the 2008 election of Barack Obama) which distrusts progress and distrusts outsiders – and distrusts science.

Just why so many Americans distrust science is hard to say. Maybe they see science as a danger to cherished values, as well as fundamental beliefs. Or maybe they dis-like its democratising power, just as conservative elements distrusted the ascendancy of human logic in the eighteenth century over divine inspiration which helped spur the French and, ironically, American revolutions. Or maybe, in common with so many people in Europe, they are wary of science's tendency to hubris – its negative associations with failed drugs and inflated claims – or the way it threat-ens to, as Keats put it, 'unweave the rainbow' and take the magic and mystery out of life. Yet, paradoxically, some anti-evolutionists happily embrace GM technology.

It's not always entirely clear just what aspect of evolution unconvinced Americans actually disagree with. When questioned, most, but by no means all, are Creationists – that is, they believe that God created all life on earth. But they are not always specific about whether they believe it was created fully formed as it is today, or whether species have come and gone, and if so, how?

One powerful element among the evolution challengers in America has come from those who promote the concept of 'Intelligent Design'. This is not an idea that has come from the Bible at all, but a pseudo-scientific notion aimed, apparently, at challenging evolution on intellectual grounds. In essence, it says that the astonishing complexity and aptness for their circumstances of most life forms on earth must indicate that they were designed intelligently, that is by God.

This argument from design is an old one, known by philosophers (and long-discredited) as the teleological argument, but the Intelligent Designers have given it a new scientific gloss with expensively funded 'research' institutes and apparently 'scientific' papers spread across the internet that trap the unwary. There have been many battles fought over whether Intelligent Design should be taught alongside evolution as a 'theory' in science lessons in American schools. The 'Designers' often, though not always, seem to win, but it's ultimately a con; it's no more a scientific idea than basic Creationism and so should have no more place in the science curriculum. It's hardly surprising, though, that so many Americans remain unconvinced by the notion of evolution, with so many powerful and persuasive voices lobbying against it.

How would you reduce crime through architecture? *(Architecture, Cambridge)*

One of the big shocks of the last few decades has been how so many of the modernistic, highly prized housing schemes of the 1960s have quickly become crime hotspots – sink estates where nobody wants to live if they can help it, and where crime is endemic. Clearly the mix of people living here can sometimes play a part, but there has been a growing realisation that the built environment plays a much bigger part. The wrong kind of architecture not only fails to deter crime, but positively encourages it.

It helps when answering this question if you know a little about a whole new approach to architecture, known as Crime Prevention Through Environmental Design (CPTED), that has become popular in recent years. Its origins lie back in the 1960s in the USA when authors such as Jane Jacobs in *The Death and Life of Great American Cities* (1961) observed just how alienating the new urban landscapes were, with their vast areas of 'no-man's land' and the lack of interaction between neighbours. It's now a major field of study that has attracted a lot of research because the implications are so important. Yet much of what CPTED promotes is simply common sense – so much so that it's hard to appreciate just how badly architects once got it wrong. It's about taking obvious preventive measures to make it harder to commit crimes, combined with more subtle measures that reduce the mentality that makes people actually want to commit crimes.

CPTED practitioners like the word 'natural'. They talk about 'natural surveillance', for instance, 'natural access control' and 'natural territorial reinforcement'. The idea is that instead of imposing military-level surveillance systems and building houses like fortresses, you exploit thoughtful design so that neighbourhoods become naturally self-policing, and access is discouraged. It's about building a sense of ownership and community so that people look out for each other. Principles like these were used in the design of the 2000 Sydney Olympics, and they are being used in the new Buckingham and Suffolk University campuses, with lots of glass, grass and people-friendly spaces.

Crime is much less likely in settings where people are more involved in each other's lives and care about their shared spaces. This means housing must be 'human'-scale. In a large development, housing should be divided into small enclaves with a shared communal space where neighbours are likely to meet casually all the time – something which can be enhanced by landscaping gardens. But each enclave needs to be at least subtly different to personalise it, and given features such as signs and ornaments in styles that may have special meaning for the residences. The shared space needs to be attractive, too, with places for sitting, and the boundaries between shared and private space need to be soft and appealing to encourage a sense of pride and shared ownership. This shared space, and the arrangement of doors and windows to face it, may help, too, to reduce social isolation, another factor behind crime. The sense of ownership is important, and this is what CPTED practitioners mean when they talk about 'natural territorial reinforcement' – making the most of design and layout so that people have a sense of ownership which makes intruders stand out.

'Natural surveillance' means doorways and windows should look out into brightly lit open spaces so that neighbours can easily see comings and goings, who's in and who's out. This is not just a question of making it easy to spot potential intruders, but encourages a casual knowledge of who lives where, which makes the individual dwellings less appealing for criminals. Dimly lit corridors and stairwells and dark, tucked away spaces should be avoided at all costs. Hidden away parking lots and rubbish areas always attract problems. Far better to have parking arrangements in full view (unless completely secure).

'Natural access control' means using architectural design to discourage intruders, rather than razor wire and concrete. It's easy to underestimate the value of protecting potential targets architecturally. Break-ins happen, for instance, where ways of getting in are either weakly protected or out of sight. Windows and doors can be more strongly constructed and armed with deadbolts. They can also be sited in places that are well-lit and public, or, in the case of windows, hard to access. A second-floor window near a wheelie bin area, for instance, is an obvious target. But making somewhere look like a prison camp increases alienation and probably incites crime. So these features always need to look attractive and stylish, as well as strong. And it's worth creating space for planting and plant barriers rather than building a lot of walls, bars and concrete. Planting not only gives a place a more attractive, cared-for look; burglars are actually more deterred by flower beds and hedges than they are by walls. It's surprisingly hard to climb over a hedge!

Architectural devices like these are being used more and more, and police and social workers are now often brought in as consultants on architectural schemes. This is all good. The strange thing, though, is that when communities built housing for themselves in the past, they often did all this as a matter of course, without the need for consultants …

Would you say greed is good or bad?

(Land Economy, Cambridge)

'Greed is good' is what Michael Douglas said as the ruthless financier Gordon Gekko in the 1986 film *Wall Street*, as he prepared to brutally shred a company and sell off the parts. Director Oliver Stone portrayed Gekko as a monster, yet back in those Thatcher and Reagan days that kind of high-powered acquisitiveness was actually very much in vogue and Gekko was something of a hero. Ambitious young men and women aimed for the City determined to clock up their first million before they were 30. The 'loadsamoney' ethos filtered right down through society, and if few people were quite so upfront about proclaiming their greed as Gekko, they had no qualms about showing an in-yer-face, get-rich-quick lifestyle.

It wasn't simply that individual acquisitiveness had lost some of the stigma it once had; it was encouraged by economists as good for society. Famously, Milton Friedman advocated removing the fetters of regulation to allow individual self-interest to flourish. In an extreme version of Adam Smith's laissez-faire capitalism, Friedman unabashedly insisted that greed was the real driving force behind societies, and giving it full rein was the only viable route to prosperity and political and social freedoms. Deregulation of the financial markets under Reagan and Thatcher – culminating in the London Stock Market's 'Big Bang' on 27 October 1986 – was soon coupled with huge performance bonuses to lead to an explosion of the world of money.

The story is all too well-known now. Cities such as London and New York rose on a tide of money in the 1990s and early 2000s, revelling as property prices went through the roof and whizzkids indulged in a spree of spending on luxury goods such as £80 sandwiches. It seemed as if greed was very good. And then, of course, in autumn 2008, it all went wrong, as the massively overstretched banks were plunged into deep trouble, with the Midas touch of institutions like Lehmann Brothers suddenly turning to dross. As people felt their livelihoods threatened, the consensus switched almost overnight. Greed suddenly became BAD and synonymous with a cavalier selfishness that had brought the world to the brink of ruin. Greedy bankers became targets for vilification, and there were widespread calls for tough regulation to curb their wicked ways. Public anger at the revelation of the inflated expenses claims of British MPs in the spring of 2009 seemed to mark a final nail in the coffin for 'greed is good' as public figures stumbled over each other to proclaim 'greed is bad'. Even if in private people were as committed to personal acquisition as ever, few, even bankers, now feel it's acceptable to shout this out in public as they did twenty years ago.

Yet despite this apparent change, the influence of the 1970s and 80s on underlying beliefs will not be so easily dispersed. People may not say 'greed is good' but most believe it's inevitable. The rampant individualism encouraged by Mrs Thatcher, characterised in her infamous comment, 'There is no such thing as society', was part of a picture, along with the title of Richard Dawkins' groundbreaking book on evolution, *The Selfish Gene*, which seemed to imply that we are all selfish, right down to our genes. There is still a widespread assumption that people are essentially selfish and greedy underneath it all, and so there is no point in behaving as if they are not.

Indeed, the competitive individualism that came to the fore in the 1980s and 90s went hand-in-hand with a kind of paranoia – a feeling that you were likely to get ripped off or slighted if you didn't make the right moves. People become pugnacious and determined to get their fair share – even suggesting that others are fools if they allow themselves to be 'exploited'. Greed may be bad, many say, but it's a fact of life. Very few people will declare like Gekko that greed is good, but they will maybe insist that it's how we have to live if we are to survive and prosper in a tough world.

Yet the prevailing culture has a profound influence on how we all feel and behave. It's my belief that selfishness and paranoia are simply reflections of a selfish and paranoid time in society rather than an intrinsic part of human nature. Put people in a different culture and they may behave entirely differently. I feel disinclined to criticise either bankers or politicians on expenses for being greedy simply because few are better or worse than the culture they moved in. In some ways, criticism is another kind of greed – greed for a sense of superiority. But I would say that greed is bad, not just because it's morally disreputable, but because it's bad for society. A world in which people are not generous – both emotionally as well as materially – and put too much energy into acquisition is much less likely to be a happy place.

If my friend locks me in a room and says I am free to come out whenever I like as long as I pay £5, is this a deprivation of liberty? *(Law, Cambridge)*

Some friend, huh? The answer to this question must be simply 'yes'. Even with no exit fee, simply by locking you in, your friend has deprived you of your liberty. Your freedom was restricted the moment the key was turned. What matters is that your choice to come and go was curtailed. Your friend's demand for £5 before the door is unlocked simply compounds the issue.*

Liberty has long been seen in the West as one of the most fundamental human rights – so deeply engrained that most of us find any restriction on our freedom at best annoying and at worst a cause for outright defiance. 'To renounce liberty,' Rousseau said, 'is to renounce being man.' The problem, of course, is that we are not alone in the world, and so we cannot always be free to do anything we like, even in the most liberal of cultures. We cannot be free to rob, beat or kill other people, for instance. And so

---

* One other possibility is thrown up by the question. It may be that you are a young child and that your friend is the person responsible for your care. A carer may legally do whatever is reasonable in their duty of care, custody and control over a child in their care. This may sometimes include locking you in your room when you're naughty, but certainly wouldn't include locking you in to go out and party. The exchange of money to buy your freedom would suggest a very irresponsible carer and would probably give the authorities good grounds for taking you into care.

we accept that there are circumstances in which people's freedom can reasonably be restricted. Criminals can be deprived of their physical liberty by prison sentences. Those who cause offence may find their freedom of expression curtailed by libel and slander laws. It's all part of what philosophers such as Hobbes and Locke call the 'social contract' – the deal in which we give up some of our freedom to the state and in return the state maintains order. Rousseau argued that we may give up natural independence but in exchange we get real freedom.

The crucial point, though, is that the law has to specify the circumstances in which someone can be locked up – and the law also usually forbids anyone who is not legally authorised to deprive someone of their physical liberty. So although forceful abduction and kidnapping are more serious crimes than your friend's game with the door lock, by shutting the door and turning the key he or she is nonetheless committing a crime. By insisting on a payment, he is probably adding extortion to his felonies! Of course, it may be that your friend is an officer of the law who is legally entitled to lock you in a room such as a prison cell because you have committed a crime, in which case his offer to accept payment to allow you out becomes a different crime!

There are certain circumstances in which someone may be deprived of liberty against their will even if they have not committed a crime, nor are about to. The Mental Health Act of April 2009 in the UK, for instance, allows for authorised hospital staff to deprive patients considered mentally unfit of their liberty for their own good – but there are safeguards to ensure that the patient is incapable of deciding for him- or herself and so on.

In recent years, of course, the rise of terrorism has thrown into the spotlight the issue of how long a suspected criminal can be detained by the authorities without a trial and whether, for the safety of society, it's right to deprive of their liberty someone who might in future commit a crime but has not done so yet. The fears of what terrorists may do has definitely swung more people behind a willing trade-off of freedom to reduce the dangers, and yet the US government came under fire in the Bush era for the long-term detention without trial in Guantanamo Bay of people suspected of terrorist links. In 2008, the UK government pushed to extend the time that terrorist suspects could be detained before they were either released or brought to trial from 28 to 42 days. After fierce opposition in the House of Lords, they were forced to accept that this extension could only be allowed under specially introduced short-term emergency legislation.

It's easy to say that we can lock people up when they've done wrong. The problem is that not everyone agrees just what is right and what is wrong. That's why the great nineteenth-century philosopher John Stuart Mill argued in his 1859 book *On Liberty* that right and wrong are irrelevant; the only justification for any restriction on individual liberty is to prevent harm to others. By Mill's argument, it doesn't matter if nearly everyone considers something immoral; it should never be restricted by law if no one is harmed by it. There was a famous legal debate in the 1960s between H.L.A. Hart who argued that there should be no laws against 'victimless crimes' such as homosexual acts between consenting adults, and Sir Patrick Devlin who insisted that society has a right to enforce morals to prevent damage to the social fabric. Hart won then, but it remains a hot topic, surfacing in the debates over whether people should be allowed to air views encouraging racial tension or terrorism. When does their right to freedom of speech impinge on others' rights to be free from harm?

How would you travel through time?

(Physics, Oxford)

Back in 1895, H.G. Wells excited the imagination about the idea of travelling through time with his brilliant fantasy, *The Time Machine*, in which a man uses a machine to travel into an imaginary future – but no one could conceive how it could actually be done. Then just a decade later Einstein's theories demonstrated that time runs at different speeds in different places and is just another dimension of space, like length and breadth, and suddenly it didn't seem so impossible after all. Ever since, some people have wondered if we could travel through time just as we can travel through space.

Einstein himself believed travelling through time would mean travelling faster than light – and that, he said, was impossible. And yet his theories show how we are all time-travellers. As time passes, and our lives progress, we are, of course, travelling continuously along the time dimension. It might seem, though, that what we cannot do is change the direction or speed of our journey, and that's what Einstein was getting at. And yet, because time travels at different speeds in different places, we could travel through time in one sense simply by travelling through space. That this time-shift is real is shown by the fact that there is a slowing of time (demonstrable with highly accurate atomic clocks) aboard spacecraft travelling to the moon and back. So if you travelled as an astronaut to the moon, you would actually come back to earth having aged very slightly less than if you'd stayed on earth. The further and faster you travel into space before coming back, the younger you get (relative to stay-at-homes).

Recently, too, it's been found that light speed is not quite so fixed, and so not quite the ultimate arbiter of time that Einstein thought. At one end of the scale, physicist Lene Vestergaard Hau brought light to a standstill in 2000 by sending a beam through a Bose-Einstein Condensate (a gas chilled to the point where its atoms are virtually motionless). At the other, that same year Lijun Wang sent pulses of laser light through a canister of caesium gas at 310 times the speed of light so that the pulses appeared to have travelled back in time, emerging from the container before they entered.

Of course, by time travel, most people don't mean little relative time-shifts or clever tricks like this. They mean things like fast-forwarding into the distant future, or voyaging back through history to eyewitness one of Cleopatra's wildest parties, and this is where scientific theories take on more of a fantastic air. Back in the 1930s, American mathematician Kurt Gödel showed that someone could at least theoretically travel through time if they found a way of 'bending' spacetime. Spacetime is a way of describing space as a continuum including both time and the more familiar dimensions of length, breadth and depth. Mathematical theory shows that it must be curved in shape, so Gödel figured you could travel through time by taking a short cut straight across the curve of space.

To create such a short cut, you have to 'bend' spacetime, and you can do that with gravity. so perhaps a would-be time traveller might exploit the unbeatable gravitational power of a black hole. Theory links black holes to white holes (reverse black holes that spew out matter just as black holes draw it in) via tunnels through spacetime known as 'wormholes'. US astronomer Kip Thorne believes that artificially created wormholes might be just the ticket for shortcuts through spacetime. It's possible that little wormholes may be created by particle accelerators such as CERN, but for time travel, you'd need something slightly bigger – far bigger than is yet remotely practical. There is a problem, too, in that according to Stephen Hawking (who, incidentally, insists that if anyone in the future succeeds in time travelling we should have seen them coming back to us by now), wormholes are so unstable that they'd snap shut before you could jump inside. So you'd need an anti-gravity machine, too, to hold your wormhole open using a quantum effect called the Casimir effect.

US astronomer Frank Tipler has another idea that we might use. He suggests rolling a piece of superdense material into a cylinder a few billion miles long, then setting it spinning. Once it's spinning fast enough, space and time will bend around it, and if we plot a spiral course through it in our spacecraft, the moment we fly in we should fly out the other end in another galaxy and time.

Of course, there are lots of paradoxes that imply that you simply can't time-travel whatever kind of machine you build. One of the most famous is the idea of a man who travels back to a time before his parents were born and kills his grandfather. This would mean that one of his parents and he himself could never have been born – and if so, then how could he have killed his grandfather? Kip Thorne argues that there are infinite possible lines of cause and effect – each event generating multiple outcomes. If so, these paradoxes are irrelevant; when you go back, you simply start another sequence of events. Maybe you could make a quantum entangled duplicate of yourself and just teleport instantly through time and space …

Can a computer have a conscience?

(Law, Oxford)

Conscience is essentially our ability to judge between right and wrong. It's the voice in our heads that tells us that we should do this and we shouldn't do that – and it makes us feel racked with guilt if we don't. But it's hard to pin down just where this judgemental voice is coming from. It's the voice of God, many early Christian philosophers asserted. No, said Thomas Aquinas, it's simply a God-given ability to make decisions. According to Freud, conscience is our superego at work, doling out the lessons learned at our parents' knees. Many contemporary sociobiologists describe it as an evolved part of culture imprinted on your brain like language.

Wherever conscience comes from, it's hard to imagine a computer ever being tortured by guilt. As Pablo Picasso apocryphally and neatly (though not entirely accurately) said, 'Computers are useless; they can only give you answers'. And it's hard to imagine a computer with 'feelings', despite the efforts of Disney to persuade us otherwise. It may be that a computer might be programmed in future to mimic human guilt so well that it appears to be reacting guiltily. But there are two further hoops the computer has to pass through before it's going to reach that all-too-human affliction of a guilty conscience. The first is for it to be sufficiently self-aware to direct its display of guilty feelings. The second is for it to really suffer because of them. To suffer real guilt, a computer has to feel, in the immortal words of George Michael, that it's never going to dance again. Even the first of these hoops seems remote, until the best efforts of scientists can tell us a little more about human self-awareness.

However, it's much easier to imagine a computer which can, at least, tell right from wrong. Indeed, medical systems, for instance, are already being programmed to pledge a kind of Hippocratic Oath, in which they will release patients' confidential information only in certain circumstances. Just as a computer can be programmed to make the decisions needed to play chess, so it might be programmed to make moral judgements. In some ways, this is superficially not so very different from Freud's superego lessons learned from your parents, or Aquinas's God-given reason – both of which imply that the judgement-making process is supplied from without, like the computer's programming. It may also not be so very different from the biologists' conscience imprint. Interestingly, a computer is less likely to lie than humans. As Isaac Asimov says, 'Part of the inhumanity of a computer is that once it is competently programmed and working smoothly, it is completely honest' – unless, of course, it has been programmed to be dishonest.

As artificial intelligence develops, it does seem feasible that a computer might one day take control of itself. Programmed to learn and develop by itself, it chooses certain responses and extends its scope so that to all intents and purposes it has an intelligence that acts with intention. Computers have already far surpassed the human mind in some limited aspects. Some fear that one day a highly sophisticated intelligent computer which developed its own mode of extending its activities could pose a threat to humans. The worry is that biological theory suggests we humans have developed conscience and reciprocal altruism as evolution directs our 'selfish genes'. An 'amoral' computer like this could be a massive intelligence with only its own interests, and none of the saving virtues of conscience that allows humans to live together. Fortunately, such a possibility is, as yet, only science fiction.

It may be that as artificial intelligence is developed, a conscience – that is, a feedback program that makes the computer respond in a way that mimics human morality – should be made an integral part of every computer system. The program might be set out in such a way that the computer develops its moral judgements as it learns. It would be no different, in some ways, from providing a growing child with lessons in right and wrong, and then that child learning through interaction with the world.

What would happen if the Classics department burned down? (Classics, Cambridge)

I'd say the interview just might have to be rescheduled … But is this an incitement to arson? It's certainly a surprising question.

Clearly, if the department burns down, the fire must have been so severe that the fire brigade were unable to stop it. That would be quite a shock in a modern building, presumably incorporating an up-to-date fire alarm, sprinkler systems and fire doors to prevent a blaze spreading. So if the Classics department did burn down, questions would have to be asked. Why did the fire brigade fail to deal with the blaze? Were they slack in any way, either in arriving fast enough, or in dealing with the fire? Or was the fire not an ordinary fire, but started in several places simultaneously – or maybe involving accelerants, which would indicate arson?

Clearly an inquiry would need to be set up to answer these questions. If there were any casualties, there would need to be an inquest. Immediately the site was cool enough and declared by fire officers to be safe from risks like structural collapse and smouldering hotspots, fire investigators would move in and sift the site for forensic evidence. They'd also interview witnesses and retrieve video evidence. Officers of the Classics department would presumably begin checking with their insurers and begin the difficult decision of whether to rebuild or commission a new building. While decisions were being made, the department would have to make arrangements to carry on in temporary accommodation. All in all, it would be something of a nightmare.

No doubt a few people would express a silent (or not so silent) cheer at the loss of the building. The 1989 structure is not universally popular. Although it is light and airy, it is undistinguished, and has little of the elegance, simplicity and ornament you would perhaps associate with one of the world's leading centres for the study of classical antiquity – and certainly looks pedestrian in a city graced by such beautiful historic college buildings.

The biggest concern, however, is the contents, and this is perhaps what the question is after. The department's great prize, of course, is its collection of classical plasters. In the Victorian era, plaster casts of classical pieces were very popular. But in the 1950s and 60s they fell out of fashion, and many collections were broken up. The Cambridge faculty is a rare and valuable survivor. As plaster copies, they are not irreplaceable, but their loss would be heavily felt by classical scholars at Cambridge. One hopes that the fire progressed slowly enough for at least the most precious casts to have been rescued from the burning building, but there are over 400 so the chances are that some were lost.

Of course, research work, computers and data, and the contents of the library might also have been destroyed if they could not be evacuated in time. That would mean a massive interruption to the functioning of the department, and it's possible that courses might be suspended for a year or so while resources were rebuilt. There are a number of priceless books in the library, and one hopes that these could have been saved.

Fire was always a hazard for libraries in classical times, and many important classical texts were probably lost forever when the great library at Alexandria was set fire to by Julius Caesar around 47 BC. This is why it's an especially sensitive issue for classicists. Scholars cannot help wistfully speculating on what amazing works of literature and scholarship might have been bequeathed to us had the library survived – and naturally Julius Caesar is not universally popular. The starter of the faculty fire might become equally notorious ...

Don't you think *Hamlet* is a bit long? Well I do. *(English, Oxford)*

Shakespeare is so universally admired that the quality of his work often seems beyond question. Young students in particular – at least, those who have not written Shakespeare off as 'boring' – treat him with awe. So many layers of Shakespeare adoration have built up over the centuries that it's hard to see the works of Shakespeare not as a literary bible but plays written by a real person, who was prone to good days and bad. It's that hands-off approach to Shakespeare that may perhaps stifle real understanding of the quality and thrilling immediacy of his work.

The interviewer is asking what at first sight seems a quite shockingly lowbrow question. *Hamlet* is widely regarded as one of the greatest works of literature ever written, the greatest masterpiece of the world's greatest dramatist. To question it so offhandedly seems almost blasphemous. Yet the question is quite effective at stripping away the centuries of adoration and getting you to respond like an ordinary punter in the audience for the first performance in 1601 who had no sense of Shakespeare's later towering reputation, or as a modern theatregoer seeing the work of a new, unknown playwright.

One can almost imagine a pompous and naïve Elizabethan critic writing the period equivalent of: 'Mr Shakespeare has written a fascinating play about a disturbed young man who long agonises over whether to take revenge for his father's murder. Stretching the play out for well over four hours may well capture perfectly the tedium of the young man's dilatory behaviour but it really tries the audience's patience. I found myself tempted to shout, "For God's sake kill the bugger!" well before the halfway mark. Is there a possibility that Mr Shakespeare is more in love with his rambling verse than we are? (*Three stars*)'

There's no doubt that *Hamlet* is long. It's Shakespeare's longest play by far. At nearly 4,000 lines, it's twice as long as *The Tempest* and *Macbeth*. The role of Hamlet alone, at nearly 1,500 lines, is almost as long as Shakespeare's shortest play, *The Comedy of Errors*. Scholars dispute versions of the text – but with most full texts, played at average speed, the play runs for a backside-numbing four hours or more. It's perhaps not surprising that many directors cut lines for performance, believing that modern television-trained audiences with their short attention spans could not last the marathon of an uncut text. They and critics talk about 'streamlined', 'stripped down' and 'pacy' performances. For his 1948 film version of *Hamlet*, Laurence Olivier cut and pasted to such an extent that the film ran less than two and a half hours, and Olivier actually got a writing credit alongside Shakespeare. Contemporary directors are often equally brutal.

Like other film directors such as Franco Zeffirelli, one of the ways that Olivier shortened the play was to cut out the characters Fortinbras, Rosencrantz and Guildenstern. In doing so, they cut out the play's political element and made it entirely an intense personal drama. And here perhaps lies the problem with considering *Hamlet* too long. If it is too long, then what are the parts that make it too long and need to be pruned? Cut out the political, and the context in which Hamlet's drama is played out is lost – we forget that Hamlet is a prince and that the pressure on him and need for him to act (or not) is political as well as psychological. You might get a streamlined story that's easier to perform and more obviously involving for a modern audience, but it's somehow a shallower piece that tips towards the values of soap opera. Cut out the scenes with the players, as directors similarly often do, and again you get a 'distraction-free', faster-moving story, but some of the psychological and symbolic richness of the play is lost.

Of course, these stripped-down versions are sometimes worth doing for the new light they shed on the play, and because of the practical attractions of staging a shorter version. But they should never be regarded as definitive. No one can be precisely certain what text Shakespeare intended. But let's assume that the text we have in most published editions is at least close. If so, our interviewer and pruning directors are saying that Shakespeare got it pretty fundamentally wrong in this, his greatest drama.

While it's good not to regard Shakespeare's text as sacred, a dead body of work in which we cannot actively engage, it's perhaps throwing the baby out with the bath water to assert that Shakespeare got *Hamlet* wrong. Surely Shakespeare, the most adroit and dramatic of all playwrights, knew what he was doing when he wrote *Hamlet* at over four hours? If it seems too long, maybe we have simply failed to read or stage it with sufficient understanding.

There's a disturbing tendency for modern directors to regard themselves as kings of the theatre, dispensing their wisdom to barely competent playwrights such as Shakespeare, untutored infants of the theatre who are able to unlock their true potential only with the help of a decisive director. Perhaps it makes more sense to assume that Shakespeare knew what he was doing and work harder to unlock the power of the play using his own words and structure rather than simply excising them and telling a different story.

There is some truth in the argument that Shakespeare wrote for very different audiences, who had never experienced the bite-size drama of TV and the quick click of the internet, but this does not necessarily mean that modern theatregoers just can't take the full *Hamlet*. In recent years, audiences have been excited to sit through twelve-hour non-stop performances of the Greek classics. Surely it's possible for them to be equally excited by a wonderful play a third as long, psychologically and politically modern, with a cast of intriguing, believable characters, driven along not by an academic's inevitably pale translation, but by some of the most glorious verse in the English language?

Is there such a thing as 'race'?

(History, Cambridge)

Biologists have no problem being racist when it comes to classifying plants and animals. A race, a biologist will tell you, is a geographically distinct group within a species that shows its own hereditary traits, such as the maneless lions of Kenya's Tsavo national park. It's with humans that the issue becomes fraught with controversy.

In recent years, many scientists, perhaps all too deeply aware of how damaging science's exploration of race issues has been in the past, have insisted that there is biologically no such thing as race with the human species, and genetic research is backing this up. Human genome researcher Craig Venter and evolutionary biologists such as the late Stephen Jay Gould are among many scientists who have argued that there is no identifiable genetic basis to race. Genetic differences within what are ordinarily regarded as racial groups turn out to be far, far greater than those between them. Gould believed that the time human beings have been around (a mere 170,000 years at most) is far too short for genetically different racial groups to have evolved.

In fact, nearly every genetic marker studied for signs of significant racial differences fails to reveal any. Even the small things that one might expect to show differences between the races, such as blood type and susceptibility to particular diseases, do not bear closer inspection. Blood types are pretty much evenly spread within different ethnic groups and particular susceptibilities to disease turn out to be mostly geographic rather than genetic.

A race, biologists insist, must be genetically distinct. Yet the human 'races' are indistinct, with physical types blending so indistinguishably that one would have to say that everyone, ultimately, is 'mixed race' – especially since mtDNA (mitochondrial DNA), the tiny genetic time capsule inherited through the female line unchanged through countless generations, shows female ancestry can come from any racial group. Race, then, according to many scientists, is not a physical reality but a cultural and social construct, no more scientific than nationality. A very few scientists disagree, however, arguing that there are genetic differences, even if small, and those small differences are enough to mark out different races – even if they are only 'fuzzy sets' that blend imperceptibly into each other. This all matters a great deal, of course, and is not simply an arcane scientific question, because bigots make the most of any scientific evidence that there are genetic differences between ethnic groups to justify their racial attitudes.

Yet whatever science says, most of us, on a day-to-day basis, assume that race is a reality. It's a concept recognised both by the law and by the government in trying to ensure equal opportunities, and it's information requested in numerous official applications and documents. And most us of have no problem specifying our own racial type (white Caucasian, black African, Asian, Aboriginal, mixed and so on). From a young age, most of us also can quickly identify the race of others instantly by sight alone – even if mistakes are common. Regardless of what genetics shows, the physical signs of race are generally so marked that they remain instantly identifiable whatever the context. A black African or a white Caucasian is still identifiable as such even if brought up in a completely different racial context, which is why it's not enough to say that race is a 'social and cultural construct'. However defined, it is a reality.

If your race is in the majority in the place where you live, you might easily forget issues of race, or even that race exists (in whatever form), but if you are in a minority you are constantly reminded of the differences. Sometimes, these are something to celebrate. But sometimes they can bring great suffering.

What matters more, perhaps, than the reality of such ethnic differences is our attitude towards them. No one likes being labelled, and race is one of the most powerful and dangerous of all labels.

Is nature natural? *(Geography, Oxford)*

Three simple words in this question – yet what a web they create. Today, the word 'nature' is used readily as a blanket term for the 'natural' world around us without necessarily defining exactly what is meant. Or it might describe something's essential qualities, their inner or true nature. That's the sense the Ancient Greeks would have understood, and the Roman origins of the word *natura* meant 'birth' – and described qualities that things were born with. Some things, the Greeks believed, are inborn – formed by nature – and some are added by man. Aristotle summed it up neatly: 'Art completes what nature cannot finish.'

Art and nature were seen as complementary opposites, and until a few hundred years ago that's how most people saw it. The seventeenth-century author Thomas Browne thus would have had a simple answer to the question 'Is nature natural?' Browne wrote in *Religio Medici* (1643): 'Now nature is not at variance with art, nor art with nature; they being both the servants of his providence. Art is the perfection of nature. Were the world now as it was the sixth day, there were yet a chaos. Nature hath made one world, and art another. In brief, all things are artificial; for nature is the art of God.' Most of his contemporaries would have concurred.

Over the next two centuries ideas shifted, however. When the Victorian poet Philip James Bailey wrote, 'Art is man's nature; Nature is God's art', it might seem to be saying the same thing as Browne, but Browne would not have understood what he meant, nor its punning style. To Browne and his time, nature was simply all the physical world – created by God, not by man – and those who tried to understand how it works were described as 'natural philosophers'. But to the Victorians there was nature, which meant little more than 'characteristics', and there was Nature, with a capital 'N' – the big outdoors which keen Victorian naturalists went out and studied in the countryside, and romantic poets waxed lyrical about.

Nature had become separated from the sphere of man's activities and interests, and was no longer the complementary opposite of art. Natural philosophers became 'scientists' and those professionals who studied plants and animals were botanists and zoologists. Naturalists were merely amateurs who made a hobby of observing birds and butterflies, wildflowers and mosses and so on. More and more, Nature became what it is today – something we enjoy in lavish TV documentaries and on trips to the countryside, or in school activities, but are never really part of. In fact, Nature is something that doesn't come naturally, any more than an interest in computers or cooking. In this sense, Nature has become unnatural.

But there is a whole other side to this question – just how much the natural environment is actually natural. Nearly every inch of the landscape of the English country-side, for instance, is the product of thousands of years of human toil, and the wild plants and creatures of the fields are those that have adapted to this man-made landscape – birds such as the skylark and corn bunting, linnet and grey partridge; rodents such as field mice; and meadow flowers such as cowslips and trefoil, scabious and daisy. And as modern intensive farming practices further alter the land-scape, many of these ancient farmland species have in turn come under threat, like their natural forebears in the past. Wild cowslips have almost had their day; now it's the age of nettles.

And what is true in England is true globally. Human activity has significantly altered the natural environment all over the world, not just by creating farmland from what was once virgin forest or plain, but by polluting the atmos-phere and water and much more besides. Countless spe-cies of wildlife have been endangered in what seems like a massive cull as their habitat has been altered or destroyed altogether.

Yet though many species will die out, others will thrive. Nature will not die out but just alter its course. On the whole, human activity tends to reduce diversity but allows a few successful species to flourish, often to pest proportions.

And of course even the crops and livestock that humans fill the landscape with are actually the descendants of native plants and animals. So however much it's altered by human activity, nature, or rather the natural environment, can always be described as natural.

Of course, we humans are actually a product of nature ourselves. So even the most extreme man-made environments, from a Shanghai shopping mall to a nuclear bunker, could be described as natural. If, however, your definition of natural is 'unaltered by humans', then there is virtually no corner of the planet which could be described as natural ...

In recent years, the word 'natural' has acquired the aura of angels. Everything from GM foods to women pregnant at 65 has been labelled 'unnatural' by their opponents, as if that is enough to damn them forever, while advertisers can put a positive spin on just about anything by describing it as 'natural' (presumably untainted by the 'dangerous' input of scientists and manufacturers). In one of those jaw-clenching ironies, an orange tart labelled as full of 'natural orange flavour' has almost certainly never been near an orange, natural or unnatural. Food retailers can legally label food as 'naturally flavoured' if the cocktail of chemicals it contains creates a taste that just vaguely resembles the real thing.

Yet just why is natural so easily seen as good and unnatural bad? After all, diseases such as malaria and cholera are natural. In fact, death is quite natural, too. I'd guess it's in part a hangover from the ancient belief that things in their proper, natural form were, in their way, perfect, and, in Christian times, reflections of God's creation. Unnatural things were distortions of these perfect forms created by the devil. When people talked about 'unnatural acts' they were talking about something a lot nastier than making 'natural strawberry flavour' drinks from chemicals.

Yet that ancient prejudice has been revived and reinforced beyond measure in the modern world by the distrust provoked by big manufacturing companies and agribusinesses, scientists and food technologists. This distrust is founded on genuine real disasters, from eugenics to thalidomide and from Hiroshima to Chernobyl. 'Natural' by contrast seems to be safe, tried-and-tested over millions of years. It's free from dangerous artifice, human hubris and the taint of big money. In this sense, nature is always natural.

> *There is a pleasure in the pathless woods,*
> *There is a rapture on the lonely shore,*
> *There is society, where none intrudes,*
> *By the deep sea, and music in its roar:*
> *I love not man the less, but Nature more.*
> Lord Byron, *Childe Harold's Pilgrimage* (1812–18)

Is the environment a bigger crisis than poverty/AIDS etc? *(Land Economy, Cambridge)*

Of course, this partly depends on who you are. If you're someone whose family is afflicted by AIDS then clearly that's the biggest crisis. If you're one of the billions of people around the world living in extreme poverty, then that is the biggest crisis. If you're someone whose traditional way of life has been ruined by the destruction of rainforest, then that's the biggest crisis.

But looking at these problems on a global scale, the most massive immediate problem is clearly poverty. The number of people – more than a third of the world's population – suffering miserable lives or worse as a result of poverty around the world is huge and unacceptable. 4.4 billion people live in developing countries. Three-fifths lack basic sanitation. Almost one third have no access to clean water. A quarter do not have adequate housing. A fifth have no access to modern health services. A fifth of children do not make it to the end of primary school. A fifth are continually ill because they do not have adequate protein and energy from their food supplies. And each year, for every single child alive and well in the UK, a child dies in the developing world through the effects of poverty. There is no crisis that comes even close to this in scale, urgency or tragedy. It's a calamity for humanity, and demands immediate attention.

The damage to the environment is potentially cata-strophic. If, for instance, global warming is even half as bad as some of the worst scenarios predict, it could be devastating. Many of the world's great cities could be drowned by rising seawater as ice caps melt and the oceans warm and swell. Many productive areas of farmland could be turned to desert by drought. And the extra energy in the atmosphere could generate storms that wreak havoc around the world. In future, environmental damage could do untold, irreparable harm to life on earth that lasts for many generations, if not forever. So in the long term, the threat of destroying our planet must be considered a bigger problem than poverty. However, poor people need help now. For them, the threats to the planet in a few decades' time make no difference; most of them will not be alive to see it unless their problems are addressed now.

Of course, it's absurd rating crises like this. They are the most serious issues facing humanity and all demand attention. What's more, they are not separate problems to be packaged up and dealt with one by one. They are intimately related in both cause and effect, and they need to be dealt with together. AIDS, for instance, often goes hand-in-hand with poor living conditions and a lack of education, both of which are also closely linked to poverty. And poverty, of course, is often a direct result of environmental problems, and the poorest of the poor are likely to be the worst hit by the effects of climate change – such as impoverished inhabitants in low-lying Bangladesh as sea levels rise, and the peoples of the Sahel as the desert expands. But the interconnectedness goes much deeper, and it's almost inconceivable that we could 'solve' one without addressing the others.

On a very superficial level, the main threats to the environment are a direct result of intensive economic development around the world, but especially in the developed countries. Massive energy consumption and massive demand for resources (mineral, water, food and land) put huge pressure on the environment. Poverty is essentially the counter side of the concentration of energy and resources into the world's economic hotspots. Economists and development experts have many ideas how it could and should be done, but it seems likely that both world poverty and environmental damage could be alleviated by damping down the furnace of consumption in the economic hotspots and working to spread a more even, sustainable level of development around the world.

Why do the words 'God' and 'I' have capital letters? (Oriental Studies, Cambridge)

This is presented as if it's a difficult or controversial question, maybe about the status of religion. After all, some of us were told at school that God is capitalised out of respect for the Almighty. But it's just a diversion. The answer is quite simple: in English, proper names are always given an initial capital letter, and God is a proper name, just as Gordon and Barack are. The word 'God' should still be capitalised even if you have no respect, providing you are referring to the being known as God – in other words, when the being's proper name is God.

So even an atheist should capitalise God, although he has no more belief in God than he does in Puff the Magic Dragon. You might split hairs if you were a particularly tricky kind of atheist and try to say that because you don't believe he exists he can't have a proper name, but you'd be wrong because possession of a proper name is not a proof or even acceptance of something's existence, any more than Superman's is.

But the word 'god' should not have a capital, of course, if it's used descriptively rather than as a proper name – when you're referring to just any god, or one of the gods, or a real goddess. The word 'I' is the only personal pronoun to be capitalised, and it may simply be that the single letter 'i' would look insufficient in lower case.

The grey area would seem to arise, perhaps, when you use personal pronouns for God, but you would use capitals when referring to His Majesty, or His Holiness, so it may be right to insist on capitalising Him when referring to God, regardless of respect, because Him could be used as a title, not a personal pronoun. I think, though, that most people accept a lower case 'him' is the norm nowadays.

The distinction between capitals and non-capitals or, in printing terminology, upper and lower case, emerged only in the Middle Ages in European languages. (The letters are called upper case and lower case because in the days of movable type, the capital (majuscule) letters literally came from the upper case or tray of letters and the small (minuscule) letters from the lower case.) In classical texts, all letters were capitals. The rules for usage vary with each language, and have varied through history. All European languages begin sentences and lines in verse with capitals (although a few modern poets have deliberately subverted the rule), but within sentences and lines usage varies. In German, every proper noun is given a capital, and that was once true of English. Now only specific names and things such as adjectives derived from nouns (e.g. Newtonian physics) have capitals.

Is it more important to focus on poverty at home or poverty abroad?

(Land Economy, Cambridge)

Very few people would deny that poverty is an issue that demands attention. No politician could credibly stand up in parliament, for instance, and assert that it isn't important – however vacillating he or she might be in actually doing anything about it. It's one of the major issues facing the world today.

The scale of devastation wreaked by poverty around the world is truly appalling. There are over a billion people – a fifth of the world's population – living in what the World Bank calls 'extreme poverty' and a further 1.6 billion living in what they call 'moderate poverty', the vast majority of these in sub-Saharan Africa and in India. The definition of 'extreme poverty' is living on less than a dollar day – and that means perpetual malnourishment, no proper home and an exposure to disease and deprivation that at best causes misery, and at worst death. And there is little moderation in 'moderate poverty', which means struggling to exist on less than $2 a day. Today's newspapers could print the headline 'Yesterday, 25,000 children died from extreme poverty around the world', and they could print the same every day of the year, year in year out, and it would still be true. But of course most die invisibly, far away from the attention of the world's media, with only a few of the worst crises making the news.

The effects of poverty 'at home' are less extreme than they may be in the developing countries. Oxfam's definition of poverty in the UK means living on less than 60 per cent of the median income after housing costs are deducted (£108 per week for a single adult in 2006). That may not sound so terrible compared to poverty in sub-Saharan Africa, but it still brings misery – never having enough to eat well, rarely being warm in winter, never affording the small pleasures that make life bearable.

Most people would agree that the suffering all this poverty causes is unacceptable. For us to live affluently while others suffer and starve is not only morally dubious, but ultimately corrosive of our own well-being. And yet, global poverty has, if anything, got worse in the last few decades. If it weren't for the enormous strides forward in China, many more people would have slipped into the poverty trap around the world than have climbed out of it. Even in the UK, the government's earnest and genuine pledges to reduce child poverty at home seem to have run backwards. This is all the more distressing in view of the fact that there have been several high-profile international resolutions to tackle global poverty – most notably at the G8 conference in Gleneagles in 2005, when Tony Blair, backed by a chorus of rock concerts around the world, cajoled the world's richest nations into pledging £25 billion of aid to Africa by 2010.

The outcome of that Gleneagles pledge is perhaps symptomatic of why there is such scant progress. Of the eight nations who pledged money in 2005, only Britain has kept its promises, while Italy, France and Japan have fallen way short, despite pressure from Gordon Brown and Barack Obama at the L'Aquila G8 summit in Italy in July 2009. It looks almost certain that Africa will get much less than a third of the promised aid by next year's deadline. When you realise that this meagre target was just 5 per cent of what the USA spends on defence, and just 2 per cent of what the UK government alone put into bailing out failing banks in the 2009 crisis, it becomes clear why there is no movement on world poverty. If governments such as France's have so little financial freedom of movement that they cannot even come up with what was, in any case, a token sum, then it's clear that high-profile international efforts will achieve little.

The amounts of money in circulation around the world, the imbalance of which is really behind poverty both at home and abroad, is astronomical compared to the amounts international bodies are tinkering with when they discuss aid. The 2009 bank bailout cost the US government $23 trillion dollars – that's well over 10,000 times the entire GDP of a country like Gambia, and many hundreds of times the GDP of the whole of Africa. This is not to say the US government should have sent the money to Africa instead (though maybe they should have); they would say, and perhaps they're right, that while they can move that mountain of cash into the banking system to support the US economy, even a tiny increase in donations to Africa causes major problems.

The gob-smacking scale of these differences makes absolutely clear the utter powerlessness of governments, or individual aid organisations, to have much impact in the face of the real international movements of money on the global scale.* The economic disparities in the world are created by the unseen movement of literally quadrillions of

---

* I am not saying, by any means, that such efforts are meaningless. Far from it. People need help, now, and aid can make an immense difference to the lives of individuals. Indeed, it's important because it's one of the ways each one of us can make a difference now. I may be talking about the problems of finding a long-term global solution, but people who are living on the edge need something more immediate.

dollars by the world financial system and global corporations. This is why there are so many poor people both at home and abroad.

So when it comes to focusing on poverty at home or abroad in the long term, it's clear that this is something of a red herring. They have both the same root cause and the same ultimate solution, which is nothing less than a revolution in the global financial system. Actually, I say 'revolution' but I suspect even a change of course might make a difference. Imagine, for instance, that the G20 governments had diverted just a fifth of the money they used to bail out banks to supporting the lowest incomes around the world. I don't have the figures to hand, but I have a suspicion there would be enough to give every single one of the world's poorest a very decent income for the next five years – and with all these extra people with money to spend, who knows what a boost to the world economy it would provide?*

---

* After I made my guess, my editor directed me to a press release issued by Oxfam in April 2009, when the bank bailouts stood at about $8.42 trillion, which stated that, 'The $8.42 trillion – made up of capital injections, toxic asset purchases, subsidised loans and debt guarantees – is equivalent to more than $1,250 for every man, woman and child on the planet. The annual cost of lifting the 1.4 billion people living on less than $1.25-a-day above this threshold is $173bn.' In fact, the bailout has been hugely bigger than Oxfam estimated. By July, the WTF were estimating that the bailout in the USA alone was up to $23.7 trillion. Worldwide the figure is likely to be over $40 trillion. So using those Oxfam figures of $173 billion, switching just a fifth of the bank bailout money could indeed lift all these people out of poverty for five years as I guessed. The

There are, of course, plenty of sophisticated economic and fiscal arguments that convincingly demonstrate the non-workability of such 'simple' remedies and why they would have been a disaster. And sadly governments and banks alike appear to believe them; they seem convinced that they do not have the freedom to make such significant shifts. And maybe they're right. But perhaps, then, it's time for a rethink …

What makes you think I'm having thoughts? *(Mathematics and Philosophy, Oxford)*

The simplest answer is: my mind. And that's not quite as facetious as it sounds. The one thing that I can perhaps be certain of is that I am thinking, and it's reasonable to describe the location of my thoughts as my mind.[*] So in a very precise way it's my mind that is making me think that you, too, are having thoughts. Whether my mind is actually right is a different matter, but it's surely my mind that is making this thought.[†]

---

total bank bailout would be worth about $7,000 for every single person on the planet. A sobering thought?

[*] This is not to say that my mind actually belongs to me (or is even located in my brain, though I personally believe it is) – I am simply using it as a label to describe the entity that is giving me the experience of thinking.

[†] Interestingly, though, the philosopher A.J. Ayer would challenge even this degree of certainty. According to Ayer, I cannot be certain that it is me having these thoughts. So I am not able to say with certainty that

Now, as many philosophers have recognised through the ages, there is no way of logically proving that my own experiences are actually real. My thoughts – the perception that I have a separate mind in a separate body – could all be entirely false. It's equally impossible to logically prove that you too have a separate mind with its own independent thoughts. However, all my life experience, all the messages that I have received from my senses during my life, confirm that things are as I believe them. I am aware of my body feeding back sensory information and responding to my commands. I am aware that things happen in a largely predictable way. Even when they are unpredictable, they seem to confirm my view that there is a real world beyond me, filled with real people who are having their own thoughts, just like me.

Philosophers have long challenged the assumptions of this commonsense realism, and tried to come up with more robust pictures of reality. They argue, for instance, that the senses are easily fooled. A fast-spinning wheel, for example, can look stationary. Moreover, how can we be certain that the waking world is any more real than the fantasy world created in our dreams? Representative realists suggest, for instance, that the mind does not experience the reality of the outside world but merely a representation of it. Idealists

---

I have a mind. I cannot say '*cogito*' – 'I think' – like Descartes, asserts Ayer; all I can say is that 'thoughts are being had'. Perhaps, he suggests, it's merely the way thoughts are arranged that makes us think there is a thinker.

say that our experience of reality is all in our head, and that objects exist only as long as they are perceived. It's a conundrum which philosophers have yet to resolve.

However, even though as a philosopher it's fascinating – indeed fundamental – to explore questions like these, for everyday practical life it makes sense to go with the com- monsense view, which accepts our experience as real. In fact, I find it almost impossible to think and live any other way, because that's the way my mind works. So I live as if the evidence of my experience and my senses is true, and that you are another human being, with a mind just like mine, and that you are having thoughts just like me. So that's what 'makes' me think you are having thoughts.

Of course, I could be wrong in another way. Your body may be a physical reality, but what you do and what you say may not necessarily come from your thoughts. You may be simply a very realistic android, programmed to give very convincing responses ... But if you are such an android, you're a pretty believable one, so I think that it might make sense to hedge my bets and assume that you are a thinking human being and not a duplicitous dummy ...

So Who's Clever Now?

Think again ...

Well, it's been quite a ride, hasn't it? We've been probing inside the mind of a snail, falling through the centre of the earth, voyaging on Noah's ark, delving into the nuances of girl scouting, and strutting the stage with Shakespeare, and so many other places! I hope you've found it stimulating. I know I have. These questions really make you think, don't they? I'm sure that no one will agree with my answers. If I look back at them I know I would myself answer things differently second time round. But I hope they will at least have got you thinking.

There is a genuine excitement in really thinking, in exercising one's intellect, that too often gets forgotten after student days. We enjoy challenging ideas, playing games with them, and, if we are honest, showing off just how clever we are – briefly illuminating the dreariness of the world with our flashes of intellectual mastery ...

Cleverness can be captivating, both for those who dole it out and those who witness it. Sometimes a dazzling display of erudition and wit can be as entertaining and uplifting as a great piece of music. And maybe some of you who read these questions will be spurred to such heights. Maybe you even imagine yourself confronting those probing Oxbridge admissions tutors and slaying them with the sheer brilliance of your answer.

But of course, if you're not careful, you might just get up people's noses. As Samuel Johnson said, 'There is nothing that exasperates people more than a display of superior ability or brilliance in conversation. They seem pleased at the time, but their envy makes them curse the conversationalist in their heart.'

And with his normal scintillating accuracy, Oscar Wilde homed in on an even greater danger. In *A Woman of No Importance*, Lady Hunstanton neatly puts the brilliant Mrs Allonby in her place: 'How clever you are, my dear. You never mean a single word you say!'

Maybe you came up with wonderful clever answers to some of these questions. Maybe you were provoked to come up with some important new ways of thinking on serious issues. Or maybe you were just provoked. Or simply befuddled. If so, there's no better recipe than that of W.C. Fields, who asserted: 'If you can't dazzle them with brilliance, baffle them with bull.'